Peter Rawcliffe, MD graduated from Pembroke College, Cambridge, and carried out his clinical studies at the London Hospital in Whitechapel. He subsequently worked in the Gastroenterology Unit at the Hammersmith Hospital, London and in 1979 moved to the Radcliffe Infirmary, Oxford. Here he has been involved in research into celiac sprue and in particular in trying to define more closely the damaging components of wheat gluten. He runs a clinic with Ruth Rolph for about seventy celiac patients. His main interests are fly-fishing and gardening.

Ruth Rolph gained an honors degree in nutrition from Queen Elizabeth College, London University, in 1975. Following State Registration, she became a dietitian in Oxford and has developed a special interest in diets for patients with gastrointestinal disorders. She too is a keen gardener and enjoys aerobics.

THE GLUTEN-FREE DIET BOOK

A guide to celiac sprue,
dermatitis herpetiformis and
gluten-free cookery

Peter Rawcliffe, MD, and Ruth Rolph, SRD

Foreword by
Martin F. Kagnoff
Professor of Medicine, Division of Gastroenterology,
University of California, San Diego

Arco Publishing, Inc.
New York

This book is dedicated to Maggie Stopard

Published 1985 by Arco Publishing, Inc.
215 Park Avenue South, New York, N.Y. 10003

First published in the United Kingdom in 1985
by Martin Dunitz Ltd, London

Library of Congress Cataloging in Publication Data

Rawcliffe, Peter.
   The gluten-free diet book.
   (Positive health guide)
   Includes index.
   1. Gluten-free diet—Recipes.   I. Rolph, Ruth.
II. Title   III. Series.
RM237.9.R39   1985   616.97'50654   84-14443
ISBN 0-668-05973-7 (pbk)

North American dietetic consultant:
   Karen Gunner, BSc, MSc, PDt
North American editorial consultant:
   Lee Faber

Phototypeset in Garamond by Input Typesetting Ltd, London
Printed by Toppan Printing Company (S) Pte Ltd, Singapore

Front cover photograph shows: Strawberry sponge tart (left, see page 83); Pasta salad (right, see page 43); Zucchini and red pepper quiche (center, see page 65)

Back cover photograph shows: Pineapple cheesecake (see page 83); Fruit sherbert (see page 85) with Danish biscuits (see page 99)

CONTENTS

Acknowledgments   6
Foreword   7

Introduction   8
  What is celiac sprue?   8
  What is gluten?   10
  Dermatitis herpetiformis   19
  Living with the gluten-free diet   21
  Research   24

The diet   25
  What can I eat and what must I avoid?   27
  Preparing food at home   32
  Fiber and calories   34
  Eating out   35
  Vacations   36
  Children   36

The recipes   38
  Soups   39
  Salads and salad dressings   42
  Fish, meat and vegetarian dishes   45
  Breads and teabreads   68
  Desserts   78
  Pastries, cookies and small cakes   93
  Cakes   111
  Sauces   120

Useful addresses   123
Index   124

ACKNOWLEDGMENTS

We would like to thank Dr Sidney Truelove, Dr Derek Jewell, Dr Stephen Turner, Liz Todd, and Julia Giblett for their helpful comments on the manuscript. Mrs Joan Borin, home economist, tested many of the baking recipes. We also thank everyone else, including patients and local groups of the UK Coeliac Society, who contributed recipes, or helped in other ways.

We are grateful to Mr David Heath of Welfare Foods (Stockport) Ltd for supplying us with Rite-Diet (Welplan) gluten-free flour mix and bread mixes, and for generous financial support with the photography. And to Alison Dean, home economist at Welfare Foods (Stockport) Ltd, for her expert help and advice. GF Dietary Supplies Ltd and Carlo-Erba Ltd also provided gluten-free flour.

Mrs Zena Jennings typed the recipes to her usual high standard and with her usual good humor.

1985   *Peter Rawcliffe and Ruth Rolph*

The publishers are grateful to the following for their assistance in the preparation of this book: Peter Myers, who took the color photographs, assisted by Neil Mersh; Mike Rose, for art direction, Gina Carminati for styling, and Lisa Collard and Alison Dean, who prepared the food. China lent by David Mellor Ltd and the General Trading Company, London.

The black and white photographs were kindly supplied by Dr David Ferguson (page 11, *right*), and Dr Chris Mason and Geoffrey Richardson (pages 10, 11 *left*, and 12), of the Department of Pathology, John Radcliffe Hospital, Oxford.

The diagram on page 9 is by David Gifford.

FOREWORD

Martin F. Kagnoff, MD, Professor of Medicine and Director, Laboratory of Mucosal Immunology, Division of Gastroenterology, University of California, San Diego

The dietary ingestion of wheat gluten and similar proteins in rye, barley and possibly oats results in damage to the small intestine and malabsorption of most nutrients in patients with gluten-sensitive enteropathy, or celiac disease. The same proteins also result in damage to the intestinal mucosa of many patients with dermatitis herpetiformis, although the extent of intestinal involvement usually is not as great. It is the gliadin fraction of wheat gluten that appears to be toxic. A single variety of wheat may contain as many as forty to fifty different gliadin components. Other grains are well tolerated by patients with celiac disease and dermatitis herpetiformis and are used in the diet to substitute for wheat, rye and barley.

The Gluten-Free Diet Book will be viewed as a welcome addition by individuals with celiac disease and dermatitis herpetiformis. The text first describes celiac disease and dermatitis herpetiformis and how those conditions are diagnosed and usually treated. The introduction to the medical aspects of these conditions is presented in a manner that is understandable to patients and includes a number of helpful hints for patients and their families.

The diet and recipes are invaluable for individuals cooking on a gluten-free diet. The book clearly differentiates gluten-containing foods from gluten-free foods and gives helpful advice, even regarding such items as alcoholic beverages and medicinal drugs. Individual recipes are provided for soups, salads, and salad dressings, fish, meat and vegetarian dishes, breads, desserts, pastries and cakes. The wide repertoire of new menu items significantly expands the currently available recipes for cooking on a gluten-free diet. This diversity of recipes should be sufficient to tempt the palate of those having many different dietary preferences and tastes.

INTRODUCTION

This book is for people who have celiac disease – called celiac sprue or gluten-sensitive enteropathy (GSE) in North America – or dermatitis herpetiformis, and their families. Our aim is to help you understand your condition and to give practical advice on the gluten-free diet. The first part describes what celiac sprue and dermatitis herpetiformis are and explains the reasons for the treatment with a gluten-free diet. In the second part we give guidance on gluten-free cooking and over 120 tested recipes to help you enjoy an interesting and varied diet.

A word of caution
This is not a fad diet book, nor is it intended that it should be used for do-it-yourself diagnosis or treatment. Many of the symptoms of celiac sprue can also occur in other diseases. You should not, therefore, start a gluten-free diet unless it is prescribed and you are under medical supervision. There is no scientific evidence that this diet is of any help in conditions other than celiac sprue and dermatitis herpetiformis.

What is celiac sprue?

Gluten, a protein found in wheat and certain other cereals, is harmless to most people. However, in celiac sprue it damages the small intestine and so causes a variety of symptoms. We do not know why certain people are affected in this way.

First we shall describe the anatomy and working of the digestive system. When food has been broken down by chewing, and swallowed, it enters the stomach. Here it is further broken down, both mechanically and chemically. The resulting soup-like liquid then passes through the duodenum and into the small intestine (see diagram). The upper part of the small intestine is known as the jejunum. Further digestion goes on here and the food materials, which are by now well broken down, are absorbed through the intestinal wall into the bloodstream, and so distributed around the body. Anything that is not absorbed passes into the large intestine (colon) and is excreted in the feces.

The small intestine, then, has an all-important role in absorbing the food you eat, so that it can be put to use around the body. When it fails to work properly, and food is no longer absorbed normally,

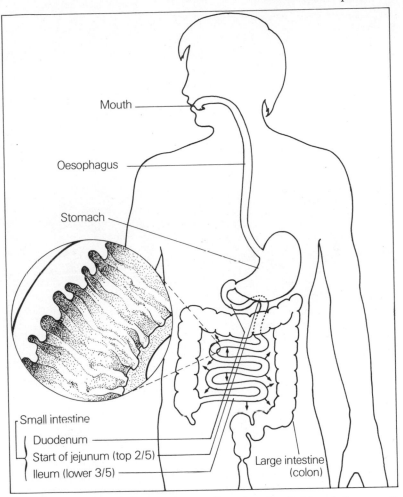

The digestive system; inset shows the circular folds of the small intestine, arrows indicate food being absorbed into the bloodstream.

this is known as malabsorption. Celiac sprue is an important (but not the only) cause of malabsorption. Malabsorption of food results in weight loss and deficiencies of vitamins and minerals.

The small intestine under the microscope
The small intestine is a tube about 6.5 meters (20 ft) long and 4 cm (1½ in) in diameter. Its most remarkable feature is that its lining, called the mucosa, over which the food passes, is very highly folded. First, the tube itself has a series of large circular folds in its surface. Next, looking at the mucosa under the microscope we can see numerous finger-like projections: these are known as villi. Each villus is between 0.2 and 1 mm long and can just be made out with the

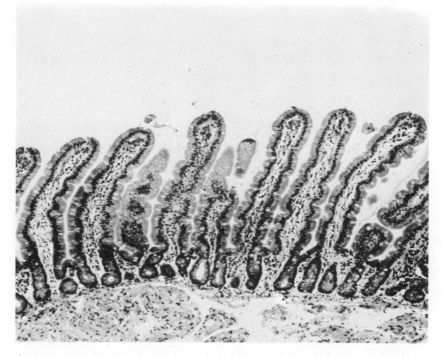

A cross-section of the lining of the normal jejunum with its long, finger-shaped villi (x 130).

naked eye. A cross-section of a villus at a higher magnification shows a covering layer of tall cells (called enterocytes), and a central core containing, amongst other things, small blood vessels. Finally, if we look at the edge of a single villus at a very high magnification using an electron microscope we can see that on the surface of each enterocyte there is a regular array of minute projections (about 600 per cell): these are known as microvilli. Overall, because of all these foldings, one on another, the surface area of the small intestine is enormous. It has been estimated that the total area in an adult is about that of a tennis court!

During digestion the food particles are further broken down on the surface of the enterocytes before passing through the cells and reaching the blood vessels in the villi. From there they are transported away, in the blood, around the body.

In celiac sprue this process is upset because there is considerable damage to the mucosa, caused by gluten.

What is gluten?

Gluten is a protein (or, more accurately, a mixture of many very

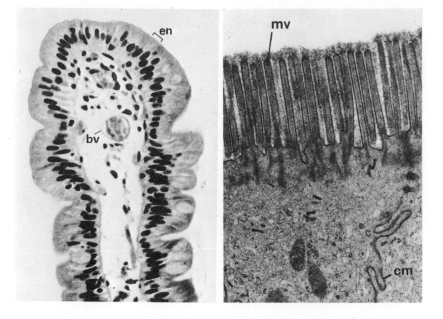

Left The tip of a villus in cross-section (x 350); note blood vessels (bv) within and the enterocytes (en) of the surface layer. *Right* Part of a single enterocyte, showing the surface microvilli (x 20,000); mv – microvillus, cm – outer cell membrane.

similar proteins) that is found in several grain crops. The main source in the Western diet is wheat. The bulk of the wheat seed or grain, which forms the food reserve for the new seedling, is milled to produce flour. Flour has two major components – starch and proteins; the main protein is gluten. This is a very sticky material – the word gluten is a Latin one meaning glue, hence the adjective glutinous – and it is largely responsible for the excellent breadmaking qualities of wheat flour, giving it the characteristic doughy feel when mixed with water.

Some other cereals have similar proteins which, like wheat gluten, are also damaging to your intestine if you have celiac sprue. Rye and barley are certainly damaging but there is still doubt about oats (see page 30). Rice and corn are not harmful.

What effect does gluten have on the intestine in celiac sprue?
In celiac sprue the mucosa of the intestine is badly damaged by gluten. You can see this very clearly in the photograph overleaf. The villi are almost completely lost, only a few small bumps remaining. This appearance is often called a 'flat' mucosa and the villi are described as atrophic. Any microvilli that remain are shortened and irregular. Not surprisingly, the result of this damage, with the loss

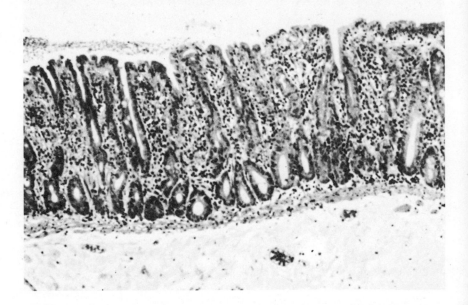

The intestinal mucosa of a patient with untreated coeliac disease. The surface is almost flat, with only the remnants of villi to be seen (x 130).

of healthy enterocytes and reduction of surface area, results in malabsorption. Malabsorption can lead to weight loss and deficiencies of vitamins and minerals. In the case shown in the photograph, the lady came to us with severe anemia due to a shortage of iron. Although she had been taking iron pills as well as her normal diet, she had been absorbing so little that a deficiency had developed.

What are the symptoms of celiac sprue?   The damage to the intestine can lead to many different symptoms. The commonest are:

Babies and children	Adults
Cranky baby, crying and irritable	Weight loss
	Diarrhea
Failure to put on weight or gain height normally	Anemia
	Tiredness and weakness
Diarrhea	Abdominal discomfort and rumbling
	Recurrent mouth ulcers
	Sore tongue
	Bone pain (due to soft bones)

People vary greatly in the symptoms they have. Fortunately, not everyone has every symptom! Any pattern can occur: some people have one of the more unusual symptoms without having any of the commoner ones. None is characteristic of celiac sprue alone – similar symptoms can occur in other conditions. We describe later the tests that have to be carried out to narrow down the possibilities, and finally to decide whether or not someone has celiac sprue.

Who gets celiac sprue?

Both sexes are equally affected and both children and adults can develop the disease. Babies may begin to have symptoms as soon as they start on gluten-containing foods when they are weaned at about three to four months. The first appearance of symptoms is common from then on until ten to twelve years old. It is unusual for the condition to start during the teens. It most commonly begins between the ages of twenty and fifty. People can develop the disease even later – one of our patients in Oxford was eighty-six when she became unwell – though this is unusual. We do not know why some people are affected as children but others don't get symptoms until later in life.

How common is it?
Celiac sprue occurs in many parts of the world including Europe, North America and Australasia. It is very rarely diagnosed in India, Africa or China. There are probably several reasons for this. Dietary habits are different and people in these countries eat little gluten. Medical care is often less advanced than we are used to: people more readily accept ill-health and so the cause may remain undiagnosed. There may well be genetic reasons too, with some races being less likely to develop the condition. Probably it is a combination of these factors, and maybe others we are not aware of.

Reliable figures for the incidence of celiac sprue are not always available. At least 1 in 5000 people in North America are diagnosed, with the probability of many others having the disease on top of this number. It is more common in the United Kingdom, where about 1 in 2000 to 3000 of the population are known to have the disease. Celiac sprue is particularly common in Ireland, especially on the west coast, where 1 in 200 to 300 are afflicted. In Scandinavia the figure is about 1 in 4000.

An inherited condition?
We have known for a long time that celiac sprue tends to run in families. Certain chemicals, called the HLA antigens, are carried on everybody's white blood cells and are known to be inherited – like the chemicals on the red blood cells which give you a particular blood group. Recent research has shown that these HLA antigens are found

in a particular combination much more often in people with celiac sprue than in the rest of the population, so it seems that a person's genetic make-up is important in the development of the disease.

However, there have been a number of cases where only one of a pair of identical twins has developed the condition. As they are by definition genetically identical, there must be other factors than hereditary ones. A difference in the amount of gluten eaten is one possibility, but in many of the twins studied the intake has been very similar, so it looks as if there are other unidentified factors.

Although the way celiac sprue is inherited is complicated and not completely understood, some answers can be given to three practical questions that are often asked:

You say that celiac sprue is inherited. If that is the case why is it that none of my relatives has it?   This is not uncommon. There are several possible reasons. First, you may simply not know enough about your relatives' medical histories. Sometimes when people go into their family history more thoroughly they do come across someone else with the condition. Second, there are undoubtedly people with a mild form of the disease who may never develop symptoms bad enough to take them to the doctor. This must have applied even more in the past than it does today. Again, minor symptoms may be attributed to other causes by the doctor as well as by the patient. Third, we do know from careful studies done on several generations of families with celiac sprue, that the condition can skip generations. Finally, the condition has been known by other names in the past, including idiopathic steatorrhoea.

What are the chances of my children having the condition?   If you or your partner have celiac sprue then there is approximately a one in ten chance that any one of your children will have the condition. As it is readily and effectively treated there is no reason for you to limit the size of your family on this account.

My child is perfectly well but is there any way you can tell whether he or she will develop celiac sprue later on?   The short answer is no. While the pattern of the HLA antigens (see page 13) gives some idea, it is not very precise. If your child has the "celiac sprue" pattern of the antigens it makes it more likely, but not inevitable, that he or she will develop the condition. On the other hand, not having this pattern, though it makes it much less likely, does not guarantee that the condition will not develop. In the future this test may be improved but at the moment it is not very helpful on its own. We believe people should not worry as long as their children are well and growing normally. Many of the routine checks done by pediatricians are aimed at spotting anything going wrong at an early stage. If your child does develop any symptoms that cause you concern, discuss them with your family doctor, who will be able to arrange tests and ask for a specialist opinion if necessary.

How is celiac sprue diagnosed?

Anyone who has already been diagnosed may prefer to skip this section. For readers who are beginning tests or who have a child being investigated we hope to give some idea about what is being done and why, and what you may expect. Every case is different, and the tests needed to exclude other conditions vary considerably. The tests also vary from one hospital to another, and are not always done in the same order. For these reasons this can only be a rough guide. If you are in doubt about what is happening, do not be afraid to ask: most doctors are much more willing to spend time explaining things than you may imagine.

Many diseases can be diagnosed without any special tests. The rash of chicken pox, for example, can usually be recognized as soon as it appears. The diagnosis of celiac sprue is inevitably slower. It starts with your first visit to your family doctor to discuss your or your child's symptoms. Your doctor will inquire further into your story asking about other symptoms, about your family and so on, and will usually examine you at this stage. As we said earlier, the symptoms of celiac sprue can be due to many other causes, some of which will get better on their own. Particularly if your symptoms are not too severe, your doctor may decide to wait and see whether this happens. If your symptoms persist, if they are very troublesome or if there are special clues, such as a family history, the doctor will next ask for blood tests to be done. Depending on what they show, your doctor may want to do more tests to narrow down the possibilities further, or may decide to send you to a specialist.

Which specialist you see will depend on your main symptoms. If, for example, you are severely anemic, you may see a hematologist (blood specialist), while you are likely to go to a gastroenterologist (specialist in intestinal disease) if your main symptom is diarrhea. Children normally see a child specialist (pediatrician) whatever their symptoms. Most people are seen on an outpatient basis – your doctor will arrange for you to go into hospital only if you are very unwell.

You will probably be given a general physical examination. You will be weighed and asked to give a urine sample. The doctor will tell you what the most likely causes of your symptoms are and which tests still have to be done before a final diagnosis can be made so you probably won't need to go into the hospital. The tests vary so much according to the circumstances that it is not possible, neither would it be very useful, to describe them all here. They will certainly include further blood tests. Ask about arrangements for the others – for example, how much time you will need to take off work, whether you will have to go into the hospital, or whether you will be able to drive home after a particular test.

You will be given a further appointment to be told the results. If celiac sprue is still a possibility you will need to have a jejunal biopsy.

Jejunal biopsy

This involves swallowing a tube with a small metal capsule at its tip, to take a small sample (biopsy) of the intestinal lining, the jejunal mucosa. The test is not painful. The arrangements for carrying it out vary from place to place. You may go into the hospital overnight (children usually do) or you may have the test done as an outpatient. Depending on the type of capsule used, and also because of variation between people, it can take anything from ten minutes to two to three hours to obtain satisfactory specimens. The test is usually done by a doctor but in some larger hospitals where many biopsies are carried out a specialist nurse does it.

You will not be put to sleep. The doctor may decide to give you a mild sedative beforehand though most people get along very well without one. In the case of young children a strong sedative is prescribed. The back of your throat may be sprayed with a local anesthetic immediately before the test. If so, you should not eat or drink afterwards until the effects of the spray have completely worn off: the doctor carrying out the test will tell you about this but if you are unsure, ask.

During the test the position of the tube in your intestine will be checked by X-ray. For women of childbearing age it is usual to arrange the test at a time when they cannot be pregnant, even without knowing, as X-rays can be harmful to the baby. This means that the test is done during the ten days immediately following the start of a menstrual period. If you have any reason to think that you may be pregnant then of course you must let your doctor know. But if you are very certain that you could not be pregnant and there is some urgency to get on with the test, it may be decided to go ahead without waiting for a period. This is a matter for your doctor to decide.

In some hospitals the biopsy is taken using a larger tube known as an endoscope. Because of its size you will be given an injection to put you almost to sleep and will have a hospital bed for the day, so that you are able to sleep off the sedation afterwards. X-rays are not used for this procedure (called an endoscopy).

For either capsule or endoscopic biopsy you may be asked to sign a consent form for yourself or your child.

After the capsule biopsy you will probably be allowed to go home immediately, provided you have not had sedation, and in that case will be able to drive yourself if you want. If you have had sedation for either capsule or endoscopic biopsy you should not drive or work with potentially dangerous machinery for about twenty-four hours: the exact time will depend on the sedative used.

The biopsy will be looked at under a low power microscope and then sent for more detailed examination by a pathologist. If celiac sprue is confirmed you will now begin your treatment with a gluten-free diet. To confirm the diagnosis finally, your doctor will want to do a further jejunal biopsy after you have been on the diet for three to six months – the exact time is not important. This is to make sure that the intestine has recovered satisfactorily.

When there is doubt about the diagnosis a gluten challenge may be necessary. This simply means going back to eating gluten again after the second, improved, biopsy and then having another biopsy. If you have celiac sprue it will show damage again. A gluten challenge is very often necessary in babies and children but less often in adults: you must be guided by your doctor on whether you or your child need one.

There is no standardized procedure for the challenge. Your doctor may ask you just to return to eating a normal diet; but he or she may ask you to eat a minimum amount of bread, e.g., two to three slices each day, and sometimes to add gluten in powder form. Occasionally people get symptoms, especially of abdominal discomfort or diarrhea, in the first few days of a gluten challenge. These almost always settle down within a week or so and the challenge can continue. Symptoms are less likely if you begin the challenge gradually, introducing a little more gluten each day over the course of a week, until you are back to a normal diet. As the challenge continues you may begin to develop symptoms again – for example, you may begin to feel tired, or your stools may become looser. The time it takes for this to happen varies.

To be sure of a clear-cut answer to the challenge, your doctor will arrange for a biopsy to be done some weeks after you start it, unless you get troublesome symptoms beforehand, in which case the biopsy will be done sooner.

How is celiac sprue treated?

In the second century AD, Aretaeus, a physician from Cappadocia (one of the eastern departments of the Roman Empire, today part of Turkey) who practiced possibly in Rome, gave the first description of malabsorption. He also made some suggestions for treatment:

> In the first place, there is need of the juice of the plantain with water made astringent by myrtles or quinces. The stone of an unripe grape is also a very good thing . . . potions made with ginger and pepper and the fruit of the wild parsley which is found among the rocks.

Later authors gave similar descriptions, with even less palatable remedies. Robert Lovell of Oxford, England, writing in 1661, and quoting Pliny, says that "the hee-goat spleen rosteth helpeth the coeliack". It was not until 1888 that, in his paper *On the Coeliac Affection*, Samuel Gee of London gave the first clear description of celiac sprue as a specific condition. Gee ends his paper with the comment that "if the patient can be cured at all, it must be by means of diet". He would be pleased to know how right he has been proved.

It was not until after the Second World War that it became clear what the diet should be. Dr W. K. Dicke and his colleagues, working in the Netherlands, noticed that children with celiac sprue, who had been making good progress under conditions of near starvation during the German occupation, began to do less well when wheat and rye again became available. During the next few years it was found that it was the gluten in wheat and rye that was harmful.

In 1954 Dr John Paulley in England noticed the atrophy of the villi in the intestines of people with untreated celiac sprue (see page 11). A few years later it was discovered that the villi grew again when gluten was taken out of the diet, and that damage came back if gluten was reintroduced.

The treatment for celiac sprue is therefore a strict gluten-free diet. Gluten damages the intestinal mucosa whenever you eat it, and if you continue to eat it, symptoms develop. Even small amounts taken regularly can be enough to cause real damage. The sensitivity continues indefinitely so you will need to remain on a gluten-free diet for the rest of your life.

How quickly will I feel better on the diet?
Once you start a gluten-free diet the intestine begins to recover. The mucosa regenerates and works normally again so that food is properly absorbed. This does not happen overnight; it will take several weeks or months for complete recovery. Some people begin to feel better almost immediately, but in many cases it is three to four weeks before a definite change is noticed. A few people do not notice much improvement until six to eight weeks after starting the diet and this is especially true if you have been very anemic. You will remain well as long as you avoid gluten.

What happens if I cheat on my diet?
If you eat gluten the intestine will be damaged again and you will become unwell. In a study of adult and teenage patients, it was found that if they went back on to a normal diet severe damage to the mucosa developed in more than half within three weeks. In all the adults there was severe damage within seven weeks, though in some of the teenagers it took longer. There is of course mild damage much sooner. We know that gluten causes damage within a few hours of being eaten and repeated small amounts can add up to produce more severe damage. Symptoms are not a reliable guide to the state of the intestine as some people can have quite severe damage before they start to feel unwell. Therefore, while an occasional unintentional lapse is not a cause for alarm, you should not cheat unnecessarily. It is much safer to be strict so that your intestine is always working properly.

Other treatment
As we have already explained, celiac sprue can cause vitamin and mineral deficiences. These include vitamin D, calcium, iron and folic

acid. If you are found to have a marked deficiency when you are first diagnosed you will be prescribed an appropriate supplement, until your vitamin level is back to normal. By this time the diet will have had time to take effect and you will no longer need the supplement as you will now be absorbing enough from what you eat. Supplements are by no means always necessary, only when deficiencies are particularly severe.

When you are properly treated on a gluten-free diet, having celiac sprue will not in any way restrict you in your job, school, sport or other activities. The only difficulties that may arise are in managing the diet itself. The second part of this book gives practical advice on how to do this successfully.

Dermatitis herpetiformis

Dermatitis herpetiformis (called DH for short) is a very itchy rash that usually occurs on the elbows, shoulders, buttocks and knees, although it can appear anywhere including the face and scalp. It is not infectious. The spots are reddish and slightly raised and there are also small blisters that are easily broken by scratching.

DH is an uncommon condition which can affect both adults (most often between the ages of 20 and 50) and children, though the latter rarely. A recent survey from Edinburgh suggests that in that part of Scotland about 1 in 10,000 people has DH, but figures are not known for other areas. It affects twice as many men as women. If you have a rash that may be DH, your family doctor will probably send you to a skin specialist. Diagnosis will include taking a small skin sample (biopsy) for microscopic examination. The biopsy is taken in the hospital outpatient department. A local anaesthetic is given and the procedure takes only a few minutes.

What is its relationship to celiac sprue?
In 1966 it was found that many people with the DH rash had the same type of damage to the small intestine as is found in celiac sprue, although only about one-quarter to one-third of people with DH have intestinal symptoms, and these are usually mild. It is now known that about two-thirds to three-quarters of DH sufferers have a damaged small intestine, while in the rest it is normal. Though the damage can be as severe as it is in celiac sprue it is often less marked. As in celiac sprue the intestinal damage is caused by gluten and recovers when gluten is avoided.

There has been a great deal of controversy among doctors over how effective a gluten-free diet is in helping the DH rash, but most now agree that the rash does improve on the diet though it does not always clear up completely. If gluten is eaten again the rash tends to come back, though in a few cases this may not be for many months or even years.

We do not fully understand the connection between what happens in the intestine and the rash. Like celiac sprue, DH tends to run in families and both may occur in the same family. We know too that the HLA antigens on the white blood cells occur in the same pattern as in celiac sprue (see page 13), all of which suggests a similar genetic make-up in people with these two conditions.

Treatment: diet or dapsone?
DH can be treated with a drug called dapsone. These pills are very effective and the itchy rash disappears, or at least is greatly reduced, often within a few hours and certainly within two or three days. You will probably be started on dapsone as soon as the diagnosis is confirmed. The next step is usually to carry out a jejunal biopsy (see page 16), particularly if you have any intestinal symptoms similar to those of celiac sprue, for example diarrhea or weight loss. If the biopsy shows damage, your doctor is likely to recommend a gluten-free diet. If there is no damage, treatment with dapsone alone will probably be continued. You should use only as much dapsone as is necessary just to keep the rash and itching at bay, trying to reduce it from time to time. If you also start a gluten-free diet you will gradually be able to cut down on the dapsone. Even if you are not on the diet the rash tends to come and go to some extent over the months and years.

You may wonder why everyone cannot simply take dapsone rather than go on the diet. For some people dapsone alone is a completely satisfactory treatment. There are, though, some possible drawbacks.

- To control the rash dapsone needs to be taken indefinitely. It can have various side effects, including damage to the red blood cells which may lead to anemia. This is especially likely when large doses are being taken, in which case periodic blood tests may be necessary.

- One person in three or four with DH has intestinal symptoms or evidence on blood tests that they have malabsorption. Dapsone does not improve these symptoms or the malabsorption because it has no effect on the damage to the intestine.

The gluten-free diet can be a very useful treatment in such cases. It may take six months or more for the diet to be really effective, but by this time the dapsone can usually be considerably reduced, if not stopped altogether. Even when there is no evidence of damage to the intestine, a gluten-free diet may be worth trying especially if dapsone is causing any side effects.

There is one other drug that is sometimes used in DH – sulphapyridine. In general it is far less effective than dapsone but is sometimes used if dapsone is giving problems. Sulphapyridine can, though, also have side effects and a gluten-free diet is often a better answer in the long run.

You will have realized that the treatment of DH is not entirely straightforward. Every case has to be treated on its merits, and your specialist is the best person to advise you.

Living with the gluten-free diet

After you have been diagnosed as having celiac sprue or DH and have begun a gluten-free diet, your doctor will arrange to see you again in a few weeks' time. This is to check that all is going well and that your symptoms and blood tests are showing the expected improvement.

Once you are firmly established on the diet and all the necessary biopsies are completed, you should keep in contact with your doctor. If you move away, ask to be put in touch with a specialist in your new area. An annual outpatient visit is often all that is necessary. A blood test will be done which will show up any deficiencies that may have arisen if you have cheated, even unknowingly, on your diet. This visit also gives you a chance to raise any queries you may have with either the doctor or the dietitian. If you are worried about anything before your annual check is due you can always arrange an earlier visit.

Children
Children will be seen at the hospital regularly, especially in the early years. Babies should also be seen by the family doctor or pediatrician. They will be weighed to make sure they are growing normally, as they should on the diet. The weights are recorded so the baby's progress can be followed, and the measurements are best done at the same place each time. Older children should have their height measured as well. There is no general rule about how often these checks are necessary; it will depend very much on how the child is getting along, and the checks will be less frequent as the child gets older, but your doctor will advise you. On page 36 you will find practical points about the gluten-free diet for babies and children.

Teenagers
If you are a teenager you may find that sticking to the diet isn't always easy, especially if you have just been diagnosed. If you have had celiac sprue since you were very young it will be easier, as you will have learned how to cope with the diet over the years. As you are becoming more independent and away from home more and more, you may find it awkward and dull to stick strictly to your diet. Sometimes you may feel unwell soon after eating gluten – in a way this makes things easier as you will be less tempted to cheat. If you do not immediately get symptoms you may find the temptation to cheat harder to resist. If, though, you are still growing (and most people go on growing until they are about eighteen) cheating on your

diet can cause sufficient damage to the intestine to slow down your growth. This is because you are not absorbing food properly and you may end up shorter than you otherwise would be.

In your late teens and early twenties you no longer run this risk as your growth will be complete. You may also find at this time that you can increasingly eat gluten without feeling unwell, although the intestine will still be damaged. If you do have occasional lapses during this time and do not get symptoms you are unlikely to run into any problems or endanger your future health. Nevertheless we are not advising you to ignore your diet, only if it is sometimes particularly difficult to stick to, you need not worry as much. See your doctor once a year so he or she can keep an eye on you.

Within the next few years you will probably lead a more settled life and will find it easier to return to a strict diet to keep you fit and healthy. If you want to have children this is especially important, as the chances of your having a child are reduced if you are not well-treated on the diet – this applies to both men and women. And women who are well-treated have healthier babies.

Fertility and pregnancy

Women who have had children after starting a gluten-free diet have shown increased fertility, easier pregnancies and healthier babies when compared with women having babies before being diagnosed.

Most women with celiac sprue, whether or not they are on a gluten-free diet, are able to have children. However, fertility is reduced in women not on a diet; and while miscarriage is not particularly common in women with celiac sprue as a whole, it is more common in those not on a gluten-free diet.

Prenatal care is available to all women to make sure that the pregnancy goes smoothly and to deal with any problems as they arise. You should let whoever is responsible for your prenatal care know that you have celiac sprue.

You will feel better if you are on a strict diet. Women who do not stick to their diet often have diarrhea and abdominal pain during pregnancy.

Blood tests are carried out at intervals to make sure that you do not become anemic. There is no special risk of this if you stick faithfully to your diet, but if you inadvertently cheat on it, absorption of iron and folic acid may be reduced and anemia may result. So the blood tests are all the more important for you. To be on the safe side your doctor may prescribe iron and folic acid pills during your pregnancy. But you must still take care that your diet is gluten-free because the absorption of everything that you and the baby need depends on your intestine being healthy.

If you have to go into the hospital for any reason, when you arrive let the head nurse or doctor in charge know that you are on a gluten-free diet, so this can be arranged for you by the dietitian.

Celiac sprue does not give rise to any particular problems with the birth itself. Babies born to well-treated celiac mothers are, on average, of normal weight and are as healthy as those born to non-celiac mothers. Babies born to women with untreated celiac sprue on the other hand are, as you might expect, smaller than average.

The message is clear: stick to a strictly gluten-free diet and your celiac sprue should not affect your pregnancy. It is important that you eat a diet that is well-balanced as well as being gluten-free. Your dietitian and doctor will be able to give you any further advice that you may need. Provided your celiac sprue is well treated there is no reason why you should not breast feed.

Fertility in men Celiac sprue sometimes causes infertility in men, and this too will improve on treatment with a gluten-free diet.

Your dietitian

The dietitian is an important person to you. He or she will explain the diet to you and give you practical guidance, fitting the diet in with your normal eating habits. If you don't usually do the cooking at home, take with you whoever does when you go to see the dietitian.

Your contact with the dietitian does not finish after your first visit. He or she will be available to answer any questions you have in the future – do not hesitate to ask.

Celiac associations

We would advise you to join your local celiac association, run by and for people with celiac sprue and dermatitis herpetiformis, or your local allergy information center. Groups throughout the country hold regular meetings. Publications produced by celiac groups cover a wide range of practical and topical matters affecting people with celiac sprue and DH, including information on brand-name foods that do not contain gluten, aspects of celiac sprue, news of meetings, research and so on. A list of addresses of these organizations appears on page 123.

Similar organizations in Australia and throughout Europe provide the same services.

Life insurance

People with celiac sprue are usually dealt with fairly favorably by life insurance companies. The company will require as full a medical report as possible. They like to know how severe the disease has been and how long it has been well controlled on the diet. There may be a moderate increase in the normal premium in the early years, but this will be reduced as the disease comes under control. After four to five years of good health on the diet, the premiums will usually be the same as if you did not have celiac sprue. With this as a guide as to what to expect, if you shop around you should not have any problems in getting good terms.

How do I explain celiac sprue to other people?
People with well-treated celiac sprue are as healthy as anyone else. If you do not like to use the word disease when telling other people about it, you can call it a condition. How do you explain what the condition is? Strictly speaking celiac sprue is not an allergy in the scientific sense (where the word has a rather precise and limited meaning) but it is a useful term, readily understood by other people. Sensitivity is perhaps a more useful word.

Research

Research into celiac sprue has centered on two main questions. First, what is the difference between the intestine of a person who has celiac sprue and someone who does not? There has been a good deal of work to try to answer this question and we now know much more about the way the intestine functions, both in health and disease, yet the answer still eludes us. We do not know whether the difference lies in the enterocytes lining the intestine or in the immune defense cells (mainly white blood cells) between the enterocytes and deeper in the wall of the intestine.

The other main area of interest is wheat gluten. We are trying to identify more closely which particular part of this very complicated mixture of similar materials is responsible for the damage to the intestine. Although gluten has been known to be the cause of the problem for thirty years, we have still to discover the answer.

What can we expect from research in the years to come? How long will it take to solve these questions? It is impossible to answer with any certainty. We are sure that the problems can be solved but we expect it will be a slow process. New technological methods may come to our aid and progress may accelerate: this is not predictable. In the end, the increased understanding of both celiac sprue and of wheat gluten may produce new treatments and perhaps the development of a "non-toxic" wheat that retains the necessary characteristics for traditional breadmaking. On the way we will learn a lot about the intestine: this will help our understanding of other intestinal diseases whose origins are even more obscure.

THE DIET

For someone just starting a gluten-free diet, the prospect may seem daunting. The aim of this chapter is to show that this need not be so, and that the practical difficulties can be easily overcome. Having someone with celiac sprue in the family need not disrupt the rest of the household. Many foods are naturally gluten-free and can be enjoyed by all. The recipes offer new and interesting ideas in gluten-free cooking and eating.

Gluten is a protein found in wheat, rye and barley (see page 10). Although most of us eat it every day, it is not essential to our well-being. There are many countries where gluten is not eaten and where cereals such as rice, corn and millet, which do not contain gluten, form the staple diet. A gluten-free diet can and should be a healthy diet.

A healthy diet

Our bodies require a variety of nutrients. Fat and carbohydrate are the main sources of energy, and protein is essential for growth and the repair of the tissues. A healthy diet is one that contains sufficient amounts of each of these. Vitamins and minerals, while only needed in relatively small amounts, are also vital to many of the body's processes.

Foods are sometimes classified into three groups according to their major component – protein foods (meat, fish and eggs) carbohydrate foods (sugar, bread) and fats (shortening, butter and cream). This grouping is an oversimplification and can be misleading. Almost all foods are a mixture of protein, fat and carbohydrates and should be grouped to take account of this. The table on page 26 shows the four basic food groups as applied to a gluten-free diet. If you eat foods from each group in the recommended daily amounts, you will achieve a healthy diet. Requirements vary, according to age, sex, build and activity. The table also shows the increased intake needed during pregnancy and in childhood and adolescence. There are other foods not shown that can add variety and pleasure to eating. Examples are sugar, jams, confectionery, butter, cream, cakes and desserts. These foods are high in calories so you should eat them only in moderation. (See page 34 for suggestions on reducing calories.)

Food group	Portion	Recommended amounts
Milk and milk products		
Milk	1 cup/240ml	Children: 3–4 portions
Cheese	30g/1oz	Teenagers: 4 portions
Cottage cheese	2 tablespoons	Adults: 2 or more
Yogurt	1×140ml/5 fl oz carton	Pregnant women: 4 portions
Meat, and meat alternatives, fish, eggs, legumes		
Meat, fish, poultry, organ meats	60–85g/2–3oz	
Eggs	1	2 portions
Beans, peas, lentils	1 cup cooked	
Breads and cereals		
Gluten-free bread	1 slice	
Gluten-free biscuits, crispbreads, crackers	2	
Gluten-free cereals	1 cup dry	5 or more portions
Gluten-free pasta	¼ cup cooked	
Oats (see page 30), rice	¼ cup cooked	
Vegetables and fruit		
Dark green or yellow vegetables (spinach, broccoli, leafy greens, carrots)	1 cup	1 portion or more every other day
Oranges and grapefruit	1	
Fruit juice	1 cup	
Strawberries, blackberries, tomatoes, cabbage, Brussels sprouts	1 cup	1 portion
Other fruits and vegetables including potatoes	1 1 cup 1 medium sized	2 or more portions

Preschool children need foods from each group each day. Because the requirements change as the child grows we have not included figures. Be guided by common sense and your child's appetite. If in doubt consult your doctor or dietitian.

What can I eat and what must I avoid?

The table below shows the very large number of foods that are naturally gluten-free and which you can eat without any problem. If you look through the table you will see that many of the things you eat at the moment are included: the gluten-free diet may not be as bad as you first imagined!

	Gluten-free foods	Gluten-containing foods
Milk	Milk – fresh, dried, skim Cream – fresh, sour Cheese	Yogurt* Synthetic cream* Cheese spreads,* processed cheese*
Meat	All fresh meat, including bacon, ham, poultry	Any cooked with flour or bread crumbs Sausage rolls, meat pies Sausages,* hamburgers* Meat spreads,* pâté* Canned meat*
Fish	All fresh fish, shellfish Canned fish in oil or water	Any cooked in batter or bread crumbs Canned fish in sauce* Fish sticks, fish cakes
Eggs	Eggs	
Legumes	Dried peas, beans, lentils	
Cereals	Rice, corn, (cornmeal), buckwheat, millet Sago, tapioca, gluten-free semolina Oats – rolled oats, (see page 30) Gluten-free flour, cornstarch, arrowroot, potato flour, soy flour, chick pea flour, rice flour	Wheat, barley, rye Semolina Ordinary flour

*These foods may or may not contain gluten. Check the ingredients listed on the label.

	Gluten-free foods	Gluten-containing foods
	Soy and rice bran	
		Wheat bran, wheat germ
	Gluten-free bread, gluten-free crackers, crispbreads, gluten-free cakes and cookies	All ordinary bread, crispbreads, crackers, cakes and cookies
	Gluten-free pasta	Ordinary pasta – macaroni, spaghetti, noodles, ravioli
	Cornflakes and rice breakfast cereals, gluten-free muesli, granola (see recipe, page 78)	All other breakfast cereals and muesli*, granola
		Baby cereals* and infant foods*
		Communion wafers
Fruit and vegetables	All raw, canned, dried and frozen fruit	Pie fillings,* commercial baby and infant fruits*
	All fresh, frozen and dried vegetables, including potatoes	Vegetable dishes including flour
		Canned vegetables in sauce (e.g., baked beans)*
	Canned vegetables in water or brine	Instant potato*
		Potato chips*
Soups	Homemade soups using gluten-free ingredients	Canned and packaged soups*
Desserts	Homemade desserts using gluten-free ingredients	Semolina, packaged cake or pastry mixes
	Rice, sago, tapioca, gelatin	Packaged dessert mixes,* ice cream,* mousses,* pie fillings,* canned milk puddings,* infant desserts,* custard powder,* canned puddings*
		Cake decorations*
		Cooking chocolate*

*These foods may or may not contain gluten. Check the ingredients listed on the label.

	Gluten-free foods	Gluten-containing foods
Fats	Butter, lard, margarine, cooking oil, olive oil, fresh suet	Packaged suet*
Nuts	Nuts	Dry roasted peanuts* Peanut butter*
Seasonings and sauces	Salt, freshly ground pepper, herbs, pure spices, vinegar,* homemade salad dressings and sauces using gluten-free ingredients	Curry powder,* mustard,* mixed spices and seasonings,* bouillon cubes,* gravy mixes and brownings,* savory spreads,* sauces,* chutneys and pickles,* salad dressings*
Sugars, preserves and candies	Jam, marmalade, honey, golden syrup, molasses,* black strap molasses,* sugar	Mincemeat,* lemon curd,* lemon cheese,* chocolate and candies*
Leavening	Yeast, cream of tartar, tartaric acid, baking soda, gluten-free baking powder (proprietary or homemade, see recipe, page 71)	Baking powder*
Flavorings	All food flavorings and colorings	Beef extract,* chicken extract,* milk shake flavorings*
Beverages	Tea, coffee, fruit juice, soft drinks	Cocoa,* chocolate drink,* commercial milk drinks,* vending machine drinks
Alcoholic drinks	All except beer	See page 31 for information on beer (including ale, stout and lager)

*These foods may or may not contain gluten. Check the ingredients listed on the label.

You must avoid all food containing gluten. Remember that it can come from wheat, rye and barley, and possibly oats. Wheat flour is the main ingredient of bread and pasta and is used in cakes, pastries, crackers and cookies. It is easy to know that there is gluten in these. However, gluten is present in many recipes in smaller amounts and it is often used in processed and convenience foods without this being obvious (see below).

Oats
When you cannot eat wheat, rye and barley the question of whether oats are allowed becomes important. At present it is unclear whether oats should be included in the gluten-free diet. Most people are able to tolerate them, but a few cannot. We allow our patients to eat oats freely and only very rarely does anybody have any problems. Very occasionally someone has mild symptoms such as diarrhea or a rumbling stomach which seem to be related to eating oats. When this does happen oats are obviously best avoided. Most people though remain entirely well and their jejunal biopsies show a good recovery. This approach is supported by research which has shown, at least in those patients tested, that oats do not damage the intestine, even when eaten in large amounts. Some doctors however believe that all celiacs should avoid oats, and you must be guided by your own doctor.

Processed and convenience foods
Many manufacturers use flour not only as a thickening agent but also as a cheap filling ingredient. Its use may be obvious, in fish sticks, meat pies and sausages, or more difficult to spot – in bouillon cubes, mixed spices, pickles, spreads, or ice cream (see the table on pages 27–9). It is essential to check the label on individual products and you should avoid any containing the following:

barley	malt
cereal binder	rusk
cereal filler	rye
cereal protein	vegetable protein*
edible starch	wheat flour
food starch	

*Textured vegetable protein (TVP) and hydrolyzed vegetable protein (HVP) made from maize do not contain gluten, but if "vegetable protein" is listed, avoid it.

Remember, though, that manufacturers can change the ingredients of products, so check regularly.

Monosodium glutamate is a flavor enhancer used in many products. Although its name is similar it has nothing to do with gluten but some brands may contain gluten, so check.

If you are unsure whether a product contains gluten then it is best to avoid it. If you want to know more about a particular food product consult your dietitian or write to the manufacturer.

Alcoholic drinks

Cider, wine, sherry, whisky, gin, vodka, rum and other spirits, vermouth and other aperitifs, and liqueurs are all gluten-free. Although spirits are made from grains including barley, wheat and rye, all protein is removed during distillation.

Unfortunately we cannot be definite about beer or lager. These are made from barley, and increasingly wheat as well, and both these are harmful. The grain is broken down during fermentation but we do not know whether this is sufficient to prevent it being damaging to those suffering from celiac sprue. Beer on tap, stout and homemade beers may well contain gluten and are best avoided. It is safer to choose another drink, but if you do want to drink beer occasionally, have a bottled or canned beer or lager – it is more likely to be gluten-free, although this cannot be guaranteed. Some people are very sensitive to tiny amounts of gluten and if beer does seem to upset you, avoid it altogether.

Drugs

A few medicines contain gluten. Your doctor will be able to prescribe a similar medicine not containing gluten.

Preparing food at home

Baking and breadmaking

Where wheat flour is the major ingredient in a recipe straightforward substitution with gluten-free flour does not always work. The main examples of this are breads, pastry, biscuits, cookies and cakes. For these, special gluten-free flours have been developed and special recipes are required. For this reason there are many baking recipes in this book and all have been thoroughly tested. As with all cooking, experience is important and you may not achieve your best results at the first attempt. As well as the recipes, you will find hints and tips at the beginning of each recipe section to help you become a skillful gluten-free cook.

The special gluten-free flours now available are the result of a great deal of development by the manufacturers and have been much improved in recent years. Cakes and cookies made with them can be very good indeed. It is only fair to point out though that while it is now possible to bake good and palatable gluten-free bread it is still not like ordinary bread. This is not surprising, as it is precisely for its glutinous qualities that wheat flour is chosen for breadmaking, the gluten giving structure to the loaf. You cannot expect things to be quite the same without it.

Gluten-free flours are different from normal flour to bake with. They are lighter and "squeakier", some more so than others. There is a variety available. Some already contain a leavening agent (self-rising flours), others do not (ordinary flours). They do not specify on the pack whether they are ordinary or self-rising, so you will have to check the ingredient list to see if there is a leavening agent (baking soda, yeast, baking powder).

Many people enjoy making their own bread, but if you do not want to do this, ready-made gluten-free loaves are available. There are also bread mixes (white and brown) which provide a good, quickly made, gluten-free loaf. If you have a freezer you may find it convenient to bake in bulk and freeze what you do not immediately need.

Other flours Potato, soy, chickpea, corn, rice, arrowroot, sago and buckwheat flours are free from gluten. They are available from most health food shops.

Baking powder Commercial baking powders may contain gluten, so check, or make your own using the recipe on page 71.

Sauces

Flour is also used as a thickening agent, for example in soups, sauces, gravies and casseroles. Even these small amounts of gluten are enough to be damaging. Standard recipes can be easily adapted replacing the gluten-containing ingredient with a non-gluten alternative. For instance, in a stew, while the meat and vegetables are naturally gluten-free, the stock (if made from a bouillon cube), white pepper, and flour used to thicken the gravy, are all possible sources of gluten. Using a gluten-free bouillon cube or homemade stock, freshly ground black pepper and cornstarch is all that is necessary to make this dish gluten-free. A selection of recipes modified in this way has been included in this book and we hope that they will be particularly helpful to the beginner.

Availability of special gluten-free products
Gluten-free products are available in North America, most European countries, Australia and New Zealand. In some countries, a few products are available on prescription.

It is worth checking regularly what special products are available as new ones are added all the time. Your dietitian will be able to tell you.

Your dietitian may also be able to tell you which stores carry a good selection of gluten-free products. They tend to be the large town-center stores, but smaller stores will usually be able to order products for you, especially if you go to them regularly.

Special gluten-free products available

Flour and flour mixes (ordinary and self-rising)
Bread mixes (brown and white)
Soy and rice bran
Baking powder
Bread – canned or vacuum packed
Crackers and cookies – plain, savory, fancy, filled
Crispbreads
Pasta – macaroni, spaghetti, noodles
Semolina
Fruit cake

Fiber and calories

Fiber   Unless you take care your gluten-free diet may be low in fiber (roughage). This is because most of the common sources of fiber such as wholewheat bread, some breakfast cereals and wheat bran also contain gluten. Fiber forms bulk in your diet and helps regular bowel action, so lack of it may cause constipation. It is easy to increase your fiber intake from other foods by eating plenty of fruit and vegetables; the skins are high in fiber so eat them whenever possible. Legumes, lentils, brown rice and nuts are also good sources of fiber.

Wheat bran cannot be used to give added fiber because it may be contaminated with gluten, but soy bran is gluten-free. Try taking about 2 heaping tablespoonfuls (30g/1oz) per day divided between two or three meals. Introduce it gradually over the course of a few days. You will see that soy bran has been included in some of the recipes in this book. It can be used in many other dishes too, for example, sprinkled on gluten-free breakfast cereals or added to soups, stews and casseroles. It can also be added to gluten-free bread and incorporated into many baking recipes. It gives the finished product a speckled appearance but does not alter the flavor. With experience you will soon learn which recipes are most suitable for added bran. Rice bran is also available but is not very high in fiber (rice bran is 8–10 per cent fiber, soy bran 70 per cent fibre).

Calories   Most people gain weight when they start their gluten-free diet because food is absorbed more efficiently. This is often not a bad thing if they have lost weight as a result of their illness. Sometimes though people find that they put on more weight than they would like. It is unhealthy to be overweight: several diseases, for example, high blood pressure, coronary heart disease and some types of diabetes are commoner in people who are overweight. It is easier to avoid putting on too much weight than it is to lose it later. If you do become overweight you will need to reduce your calorie intake.

The quantity of calories you are able to eat and still manage to lose weight depends on your age, sex, height, occupation and how much exercise you get. Your dietitian will be able to give you advice on a target weight and what intake you should aim for. Here are a few tips to help you to lose weight:

1. Restrict foods that are high in calories, mainly sweet and fatty foods. Weight for weight, fats have twice as many calories as carbohydrate or protein. Not only is fat high in calories but there is evidence that in excess it has other harmful effects, for example, in causing heart disease. A few suggestions about reducing calories

in your diet, and fat in particular, are listed here. You may also find a "calorie counter" booklet useful.

- Trim excess fat off meat and avoid frying.
- Use skim milk rather than whole milk.
- Use cottage, farmer Edam, Gouda or other low-fat cheeses.
- Use low-fat spreads rather than butter or margarine.
- Use an artificial sweetener in drinks, in stewed fruit (add after cooking) and on breakfast cereals.
- Choose low-calorie soft drinks.
- Drink less alcohol. Alcohol has almost as many calories as fat.
- Eat more fiber. Fiber fills you up without adding calories.

2. Don't skip meals. Try to eat three small meals daily so you will be less tempted to eat snacks.

3. Exercise is good for you and will help to burn off calories. But be sure to start gradually if you have not been exercising regularly for some time. Do not rush into vigorous exercise right away. If you have any doubts about how much you should do, consult your doctor. Brisk walking or swimming are good ways for most people to start.

4. Above all you will need motivation, willpower and perseverance. If you cannot manage to lose weight on your own then joining a weight loss group might help you. Do not worry that you are on a gluten-free diet – the group will still be able to help, though you should let them know about it when you join.

Calorie and fiber values are given with each recipe. You will notice that a fairly large proportion of the recipes are baking or dessert recipes. We have included these because they are the most difficult to make with gluten-free ingredients – but they tend to be high in calories. So if you have a weight problem you must be careful how much of them you eat.

Eating out

Do not avoid eating out. If you are careful you should not have any great problems. If you are going to eat out and are not sure whether any gluten-free food will be available, have a snack before you go.

At friends' If you are eating at friends' homes, it is wise to let them know in advance that you are on a gluten-free diet and explain what you can and cannot eat.

At work   If nearby restaurants can provide you with gluten-free meals this is ideal. Otherwise you can either choose gluten-free foods from the ordinary menu or take your own packed lunch. Drinks from vending machines may contain gluten.

Restaurants and hotels   You can enquire in advance about the menu if you wish: you will find many chefs are pleased to help. If you cannot do this, try to eat where there is a wide choice available because you will have to choose "safe" foods from the menu. For appetizers, soups are best avoided unless they are clear; melon and grapefruit are suitable alternatives. For a main course, it is wise to choose plainly cooked meats or fish without sauces or gravy. Fish fried in batter is not suitable. Salads are usually safe but be careful about any dressing and remember that processed meats may contain gluten. Many desserts such as pastries, puddings, cakes, desserts, ice cream, tarts, pies and cheesecakes contain gluten. Order instead fruit salad, rice pudding, sherberts, meringues or baked custards, or cheese – without the biscuits!

In the hospital   If you have to go into the hospital, try to let the dietitian or head nurse know in advance that you are on a gluten-free diet. Smaller hospitals do not always have stocks of gluten-free foods so take bread, crackers and cookies with you. Not all of the staff will know about the gluten-free diet: if you are offered something which you think may contain gluten, query it, in case a mistake has been made.

Vacations

If you are staying in a hotel you will have to make special arrangements beforehand. Some hotels will provide a gluten-free diet if asked. It is wise to take a supply of gluten-free bread with you anyway – canned and prepacked breads are excellent for this purpose. If you are flying, a special meal can usually be provided, but you must give the airline company plenty of warning – most require several days.

Children

Children with celiac sprue are otherwise perfectly normal and will remain healthy provided that they keep strictly to a gluten-free diet. With babies this is easy to ensure. Many baby foods are gluten-free. When the diagnosis of celiac sprue has been made and you have started your baby on a gluten-free diet he or she will become less cranky. The baby's appetite will improve as the diet begins to work.

Give regular feeds, allowing as much as the baby seems to want on each occasion. Do not give snacks in between.

As your child gets older begin to teach him or her about the diet. As time goes by children are able to manage things more and more for themselves. Try to fit your child's diet in with the rest of the family as much as possible so he or she does not feel too different. Your dietitian or doctor will be able to help if you have any problems.

School meals

You will have to make arrangements about meals at school if your child doesn't come home for lunch. Discuss your child's needs with his or her teacher. If special meals can be provided (in the case of a boarding school this is obviously essential) you should try and arrange a meeting between your dietitian and the school cook. In any case, schools are now offering a wider choice of food and if your child is old enough to know what to avoid, choosing a varied and safe menu should be quite easy.

If gluten-free food cannot be specially provided and either your child is not old enough to choose, or there is not enough choice available, you can prepare a packed lunch. You could include cheese, cold roast meat or hard-cooked egg with salad, gluten-free crackers, or sandwiches made with gluten-free bread, plus fresh fruit or gluten-free cake. In the winter add a thermos of homemade gluten-free soup (freeze in one-portion amounts) or one of the gluten-free ready-made soups.

Parties

Do not discourage your child from going to parties. Talk to the people giving the party beforehand to let them know what foods your child can and cannot eat. If you are giving a party, then all the food can be made gluten-free.

School outings

Give the organizers plenty of warning: tell them what is needed and send food lists. Give your child a supply of gluten-free bread and cookies to take along.

THE RECIPES

Weights and measures

The teaspoon (tsp) measurement used throughout the book equals 5 ml and the tablespoon (tbsp) 15 ml; both are level.

Calories (Cals) have been rounded off to the nearest 10, as have kilojoules (kJ). Fiber values have been rounded to the nearest gram.

Unless otherwise stated, all recipes are to serve four.

Keep to either the American or the metric measurements in a recipe. Gluten-free flours are more difficult to use than ordinary flours. Accurate measurements are very important: measure all ingredients carefully, especially the amount of liquid. Because flours vary, you may find that more or less liquid is needed than is stated in the recipe – always add a little at a time until the correct consistency is obtained. Liquids should always be measured at eye level. Use the type of margarine or size of egg stated in the recipe. Molasses and syrup should be measured with a warmed spoon. Oven temperatures are given as a guide but ovens vary so adjust to suit your own. Use the stated size and shape of baking pan. This is particularly important for gluten-free baking as the flours don't have the same structural properties as ordinary flours and may need extra support. Non-stick baking paper is useful and is available from supermarkets and department stores. Rice paper is usually gluten-free, but remember to check.

Which flour to use?

Where any flour will do we have simply said "gluten-free flour". All-purpose or self-rising flour has been specified where necessary. If you use a self-rising flour instead of plain omit the baking powder and vice versa. Add 4 level teaspoonfuls of baking powder to 450g/ 1 lb all-purpose flour.

Not all plain gluten-free flours (or all self-rising gluten-free flours) have exactly the same properties as one another. Many recipes were tested with Welplan flours (sold in Canada under the British name, Rite-Diet). In a few recipes where it is possible that only a particular flour will work well we have indicated which flour has been used in testing.

Ground rice

Some of the recipes call for ground rice. This is available in North America, but may be difficult to find. You can make your own just by grinding regular rice for approximately ten seconds in a blender or coffee grinder. The texture should be similar to semolina.

Freezing
Almost all gluten-free baked products freeze well. As they tend to go stale quickly it is best to freeze them soon after making. Baking the small amounts needed for one person is time-consuming and uneconomical. If you have a freezer you can bake more at a time and freeze what you do not immediately need. We have indicated in the recipes themselves the few that are not suitable for freezing.

SOUPS

Canned and packaged soups may contain gluten. Homemade soups are good and satisfying. For convenience make in bulk and freeze in suitable portion sizes. Use gluten-free bouillon cubes or a homemade stock using any standard stock recipe.

Green pea soup

Each serving: 300Cals/1260kJ, 3 g fiber

1 medium-sized onion, chopped
60g/4 tbsp. butter
2 slices bacon, finely chopped
550ml/2¼ cups gluten-free chicken or ham stock

225g/1½ cups fresh (shelled) or frozen peas
salt and freshly ground black pepper
chopped fresh parsley

In a saucepan, cook the onion gently in the butter until it starts to soften and turn golden. Add the chopped bacon and sauté for a few minutes more. Pour in the stock, add the peas and simmer gently until they are cooked. Purée in a blender or rub through a sieve and dilute to taste with more stock. Season to taste. Reheat, sprinkle with the chopped parsley and serve.

This soup is particularly good made with smoked bacon. Dried peas can also be used: 115g/½ cup dried peas, soaked overnight, and the cooking time increased to 1 hour.

Tomato soup

Each serving: 100Cals/420kJ, 3 g fiber

15g/1 tbsp butter or margarine
10ml/2 tsp olive oil
115g/³/₄ cup potatoes, peeled and
*   diced*
115g/³/₄ cup onions, peeled and
*   diced*
450g/2 scant cups ripe tomatoes,
*   skinned and roughly chopped*

1 tbsp chopped fresh parsley
¼ tsp chopped fresh thyme
¼ tsp salt
freshly ground black pepper
1 tsp sugar
340ml/1½ cups gluten-free
*   chicken stock*

Melt the butter or margarine and the oil in a large saucepan. Add the potatoes and onions and sauté for about 5 minutes without browning. Stir in the tomatoes, herbs (reserving some parsley for garnishing), seasoning and sugar. Cook for a few more minutes. Pour in the chicken stock, bring to a boil, cover and simmer for 15–20 minutes until the vegetables are tender. Rub through a sieve and adjust the seasoning. Reheat and serve piping hot, garnished with parsley.

Cream of celery soup

See photograph, page 47

Each serving: 240Cals/1010kJ, 4 g fiber

30g/2 tbsp butter or margarine
350g/3 cups celery, chopped
115g/³/₄ cup potatoes, peeled and
*   cut into chunks*
2 medium-sized leeks, sliced
550ml/2¼ cups gluten-free
*   chicken stock*
¼ tsp celery seed (optional)
140ml/²/₃ cup light cream

285ml/1⅛ cups milk
salt and freshly ground black
*   pepper*

Garnish:
a dash of cream
celery leaves or fresh parsley,
*   chopped*

In a large pan melt the butter or margarine over low heat and add the celery, potatoes and leeks. Stir well, cover and cook for about 15 minutes. Add the stock with the celery seeds (if using) and a pinch of salt. Bring to the simmering point and cook very gently for 25 minutes or until the vegetables are tender.

Purée the soup in a blender or by rubbing through a sieve, then return to the pan, stirring in the cream and the milk. Bring the soup back to a boil and season with salt and pepper.

Serve garnished with a swirl of cream and chopped parsley or celery leaves.

French onion soup

See photograph, page 47

Each serving: 490Cals/2060kJ, 2 g fiber

60g/4 tbsp butter, plus a little extra
15ml/1 tbsp vegetable oil
450g/4 cups onions, thinly sliced
2 cloves garlic, crushed
1/2 tsp sugar
825ml/3 1/2 cups gluten-free beef
  stock

285ml/1 1/4 cups white wine or
  cider
salt and freshly ground black
  pepper
4 large croûtons (gluten-free
  bread)
170g/1 1/2 cups cheese, grated

Heat 60g/4 tbsp butter and the oil together in a large heavy-based saucepan. Add the onions, garlic and sugar and cook over a low heat for 30 minutes, stirring occasionally until the onions have turned an even, golden brown. Add the stock and wine or cider, bring to the boil, cover and simmer for 1 hour. Season to taste.

Spread the croûtons with butter and place one in each ovenproof soup bowl. Ladle the soup on top and sprinkle with grated cheese. Place under a hot broiler and when the cheese is golden brown serve immediately.

Bacon and lentil soup

Each serving: 290Cals/1220kJ, 5 g fiber

115g/5/8 cup dry green or brown
  lentils
15ml/1 tbsp vegetable oil
4 slices smoked bacon, finely
  chopped
2 carrots, chopped
1 large onion, chopped
2 celery stalks, sliced

225g/1 scant cup canned tomatoes
1 clove garlic, crushed
1.1 l/5 cups gluten-free beef stock
115g/1 1/2 cups cabbage, finely
  shredded
salt and freshly ground black
  pepper
chopped fresh parsley

Wash the lentils thoroughly in plenty of cold water, and drain.

Heat the oil in a large saucepan and sauté the bacon gently. Stir in the carrots, onion and celery, and brown carefully. Add the lentils, tomatoes, garlic and stock. Bring to a boil, cover and simmer gently for 50 minutes. Add the cabbage, and simmer for an additional 10 minutes. Season to taste and serve garnished with the chopped parsley.

Minestrone

See photograph, page 47

Each serving: 260Cals/1090kJ, 4 g fiber

30g/2 tbsp butter
15ml/1 tbsp olive oil

1 medium-sized onion, finely
  chopped

60g/3 slices bacon, chopped

2 tomatoes, chopped
1 clove garlic, crushed
salt and freshly ground black
* pepper*
1.1l/5 cups gluten-free stock
1 tsp dried basil (optional)

2 stalks celery, chopped
115g/³/4 cup carrots, finely chopped
170g/2 large leeks, chopped
115g/1¹/2 cups cabbage, shredded
1¹/2 tbsp rice
10ml/2 tsp gluten-free tomato paste
grated Parmesan cheese

In a large heavy-based saucepan, melt the butter and the oil. Add the bacon and cook for a minute before adding the onion, celery, carrots and tomatoes. Stir in the garlic and seasoning, cover and cook gently for 20 minutes. Pour in the stock, and add the basil, if using. Continue to simmer for about 1 hour. Add the leeks, cabbage and rice and cook for 30 minutes. Finally stir in the tomato paste and cook for another 10 minutes. Serve in warmed soup bowls, sprinkled with Parmesan cheese.

SALADS AND SALAD DRESSINGS

Salads are naturally gluten-free and are not fattening. But watch the dressings – not only are they usually high in calories because of the oil, but they may contain gluten. Recipes are given for making your own vinaigrette and mayonnaise at the end of this section.

Maggie's salad

See photograph, page 48

Each serving: 170Cals/710kJ, 2 g fiber

2 red eating apples, cored and
* sliced*
6 stalks celery, sliced
60g/¹/2 cup walnuts, chopped

45ml/3 tbsp gluten-free vinaigrette
* or gluten-free mayonnaise (see*
* pages 44–5)*
1 clove garlic, crushed (optional)

Place the apples, celery and walnuts into a bowl. Add the vinaigrette or mayonnaise and toss to coat the apples and celery well.
Garlic may be added to the dressing if desired.

Salad Niçoise

Each serving: 280Cals/1180kJ, 2 g fiber

200g/7oz can tuna
a few anchovy fillets (optional)
1 crisp lettuce
½ Spanish (mild) onion, thinly
*   sliced*
8 black or green olives

1 green pepper, seeded and sliced
4 tomatoes, quartered
2 hard-cooked eggs, quartered
8 radishes, trimmed
90ml/6 tbsp gluten-free vinaigrette
*   (see page 44)*

Drain the tuna and flake roughly. Cut the anchovy fillets, if using, into 2cm/1-in pieces. Tear the lettuce leaves and arrange in a bowl. Mix the tuna, onion, olives, green pepper and anchovy pieces and place on the lettuce. Arrange the quartered tomatoes, eggs and radishes on top. Pour the vinaigrette over.
   Hot gluten-free garlic bread goes well with this salad.

Pasta salad   See photograph, page 48

Each serving: 230Cals/970kJ, 1 g fiber

115g/1¼ cups gluten-free
*   macaroni*
200g/7oz can tuna
1 large cucumber, diced
2 large tomatoes, chopped
3–4 scallions, chopped

60ml/4 tbsp gluten-free salad
*   dressing, or mayonnaise (see*
*   page 44)*
lettuce

Cook the macaroni as directed on the package. Drain, refresh with cold water and drain again. Flake the fish into a bowl, add the macaroni and the other ingredients, except the lettuce. Toss, and serve on a bed of lettuce.

Kidney bean, zucchini and mushroom salad   See photograph, page 48

Each serving: 70Cals/290kJ, 5 g fiber

60g/⅓ cup dry red kidney beans,
*   soaked overnight in plenty of*
*   cold water*
170g/1¼ cups zucchini, sliced
60g/1 scant cup mushrooms, sliced
2 tbsp chopped fresh mint
*   (optional)*

15ml/1 tbsp gluten-free vinaigrette
*   (see page 44)*
salt and freshly ground black
*   pepper*

Drain the beans and discard the liquid. Cover the beans in fresh cold water, bring to a boil, and boil for 10 minutes. Reduce the heat and simmer for 1¼–1½ hours or until the beans are tender. Drain and leave to cool. Steam the zucchini until just tender and allow to cool. Combine the beans, zucchini, mushrooms and mint, if using, and toss in the vinaigrette. Season to taste.

Potato salad

Each serving: 330Cals/1390kJ, 3 g fiber

*450g/3 cups waxy potatoes, boiled
  and sliced
1 quantity gluten-free vinaigrette
  or gluten-free mayonnaise (see
  below)*

*1 tbsp chopped fresh parsley
1 tbsp chopped fresh chives
4 scallions, finely chopped
salt and freshly ground black
  pepper*

Place the potatoes in a salad bowl, pour on the dressing and mix thoroughly. Add the fresh herbs and chopped scallions. Taste to check the seasoning and keep the salad in a cool place until needed.

Cucumber raita

Each serving: 20Cals/80kJ, 0 g fiber

*280ml/1¼ cups gluten-free plain
  yogurt
1 large cucumber, thinly sliced
salt and freshly ground black
  pepper*

*small clove garlic, crushed
  (optional)
chopped fresh parsley to garnish*

Combine all ingredients and garnish with parsley. Serve as a side-dish with curry (see pages 51, 63).

Vinaigrette

Each 15ml tablespoon: 100Cals/420kJ, 0 g fiber

*90ml/6 tbsp vegetable oil (olive oil
  is best)
30ml/2 tbsp wine vinegar
1 tsp gluten-free prepared mustard
  (optional)*

*1 tsp superfine sugar (optional)
½ tsp salt
½ tsp freshly ground black pepper*

Place all the ingredients in a bowl and whisk together using a fork. Alternatively, put in a screw-top jar and shake vigorously. Any chopped fresh herbs may be added. Store in the refrigerator.

Mayonnaise

Each 15ml tablespoon: 100Cals/420kJ, 0 g fiber

*¼ tsp superfine sugar
1 tsp salt*

*2 egg yolks
285ml/1¼ cups olive oil*

1 tsp gluten-free dry mustard   *15ml/1 tbsp wine vinegar*
45ml/3 tbsp fresh lemon juice

Place the sugar, salt, mustard and 15 ml/1 tablespoonful lemon juice into a warm bowl. Add the egg yolks and, using a wooden spoon, beat thoroughly together. Drop by drop, add half the olive oil, beating well all the time. When the sauce is the consistency of whipped cream add another 15ml/1 tablespoonful lemon juice. You can now speed up the addition of the rest of the olive oil to a thin, steady stream – still beating continuously. Stir in the remaining lemon juice and wine vinegar, and finally mix in 15ml/1 tablespoonful boiling water.

Keeps well in a screw-top jar in the refrigerator.

FISH, MEAT AND VEGETARIAN DISHES

Pure spices, fresh herbs and freshly ground pepper, invaluable additions to cooking, are gluten-free. But beware of ground pepper, which can contain gluten. Take care with bouillon cubes and mixed spices such as garam masala and curry powder as they too may contain gluten. The quantities given in these recipes are usually for fresh herbs, but if you are using dried herbs, use about one-third of the amount stated.

Beans and lentils are included in several recipes. Because all beans and legumes are gluten-free and high in fiber they form a very useful and tasty part of the diet. They are high in protein and much cheaper than meat or fish, and since they contain negligible fat they are lower in calories. Dried beans, after their overnight soaking, must be boiled rapidly for 10 minutes before simmering until soft.

Rice is gluten-free. Brown rice has more flavor than white rice and more fiber, vitamins and minerals. When cooking any type of rice always follow the instructions on the package. As a general rule use 1 cup rice to 2 cups water with a level teaspoon of salt. But some brown rice may need more water and takes longer to cook.

Vegetables are also useful sources of fiber yet low in calories. They contain lots of vitamins and minerals. Do not overcook as this destroys a lot of the goodness. Potatoes are not as fattening as many people think, though adding butter to them when mashing, or frying them will greatly increase the calories. The skins are high in fiber, so scrub or scrape them rather than peeling and boil or bake them in their skins.

Although meat and fish are naturally gluten-free, when they are cooked in casseroles or served with sauces or with gravy, you must take care not to introduce gluten – for example, thicken them with cornstarch or gluten-free flour, as in these recipes, rather than with ordinary flour.

Meat is a good but expensive source of protein. However, even lean meat contains quite a lot of fat and so is high in calories. To reduce the fat content trim off any visible fat and broil or braise rather than sauté. Fish is less fatty, but again avoid frying – broil, steam, bake or poach.

FISH

Fisherman's pie

Each serving: 400Cals/1680kJ, 2 g fiber

450g/1 lb fresh cod, skinned
salt and freshly ground black
  pepper
1 bay leaf
450g/3 cups Idaho potatoes, peeled
45g/3 tbsp butter
170ml/²/₃ cup milk
30g/4 tbsp gluten-free flour

2 hard-cooked eggs, chopped
grated rind of 1 lemon
15ml/1 tbsp lemon juice
¼ tsp cayenne pepper
1 tbsp chopped chives
1 tbsp chopped fresh parsley
30g/1¼ cup Cheddar cheese,
  grated

Pre-heat the oven to 375°F/190°C.

Poach the fish in water, seasoned with salt, black pepper and the bay leaf, for 10–15 minutes. Drain and reserve 140ml/¹/₃ cup of the cooking liquid. Boil the potatoes and mash them with 15g/1 tbsp butter and 30ml/2 tbsp of the milk. Melt the remaining butter in a saucepan, add the flour and cook for a few more minutes, stirring. Gradually stir in the remaining milk and the reserved fish stock. Bring to a boil, stirring continuously, to make a fairly thick white sauce. Flake the fish and add it to the sauce with the chopped eggs, lemon rind and juice, cayenne pepper, chives and parsley. Season to taste. Turn into a 9-in. pie plate. Sprinkle with the grated cheese. Spoon or pipe the mashed potato over the fish mixture and bake for 20–30 minutes.

Cream of celery soup (*top*, see page 40); Minestrone (*left*, see page 41); French onion soup (*right*, see page 41)

Trout in oatmeal

Each serving: 520Cals/2180kJ, 2 g fiber

4 trout
salt and freshly ground black
pepper

60g/¹/₂ cup fine or medium
oatmeal (see page 30)
60g/4 tbsp butter
lemon wedges

Ask the fish market to clean the fish and fillet them by splitting them down the back or do it yourself. Season to taste with salt and pepper. Coat both sides with oatmeal. Sauté in the butter until cooked through and lightly browned.

Serve garnished with the lemon wedges.

Baked stuffed mackerel   See photograph, page 59

Each serving: 330Cals/1390kJ, 6 g fiber

4 mackerel
salt and freshly ground black
pepper
1 medium-sized cooking apple
1 medium-sized onion, finely
chopped

60g/1 cup gluten-free bread
crumbs
30g/¹/₂ cup soy bran
2 tsp sugar
30g/2 tbsp butter, melted

Preheat the oven to 350°F/180°C. Grease an ovenproof dish.

Clean and bone the mackerel or have it done by the fish market. Sprinkle with salt and pepper and set aside. Pare, core and grate the apple, mix with the onion, two-thirds of the bread crumbs, and the bran, sugar, salt and pepper. Place some stuffing in each fish and fold over. Place in the greased dish, sprinkle with the rest of the bread crumbs and pour the melted butter over. Bake uncovered for 20–25 minutes or until the fish is tender.

Smoked fish pâté   See photograph, page 58

Serves 8

Each serving: 150Cals/630kJ, 0 g fiber

2 medium-sized smoked mackerel
(or other smoked fish)
140 ml/²/₃ cup sour cream
115g/¹/₂ cup cottage cheese
juice of ¹/₂ lemon
salt and freshly ground black
pepper

pinch freshly grated nutmeg

Garnish:
lemon wedges
watercress
pinch cayenne pepper

Maggie's salad (*top*, see page 42); Kidney bean, zucchini and mushroom salad (*center*, see page 43); Pasta salad (*bottom*, see page 43)

Skin the mackerel and remove the bones. Flake the fish and put in a bowl. Add the sour cream, cottage cheese and lemon juice and beat with a wooden spoon until smooth; or place all ingredients in a blender and blend until completely smooth. Season, add the nutmeg and a little more lemon juice if necessary. Chill for several hours.

Sprinkle a pinch of cayenne pepper on top and serve garnished with lemon wedges and watercress accompanied by hot gluten-free toast.

Fish cakes

See photograph, page 58

Makes 12

Each fish cake: 150Cals/630kJ, 0 g fiber

*450g/2 cups boiled, mashed
   potatoes,
450g/1 lb cod poached, skinned
   and well-drained
3 tbsp chopped fresh parsley
5ml/1 tsp gluten-free anchovy
   paste
1 egg, beaten
10ml/2 tsp lemon juice
a little freshly grated nutmeg*

*good pinch cayenne pepper
salt and freshly ground black
   pepper*

*For coating:
2 eggs, beaten
170g/1½ cups dry gluten-free
   white bread crumbs
45–60ml/3–4 tbsp vegetable oil
knob of butter*

Mix together the fish cake ingredients in a large bowl. Adjust seasoning.Refrigerate for an hour or so, until the mixture is firm. Turn out on to a board dusted with gluten-free flour and lightly work into a roll about 5cm/2-in diameter. Cut the roll into 12 slices. Dip each into the beaten egg and coat with bread crumbs. Heat the oil and butter together in a skillet and shallow fry the fish cakes until golden. Drain on kitchen towels and serve immediately.

Tartare sauce or parsley sauce go well with these fish cakes (see pages 120, 122).

Kedgeree

Each serving: 410Cals/1720kJ, 1 g fiber

*675g/1½ lb smoked or fresh
   haddock
225g/1 cup long-grain white or
   brown rice
85g/6 tbsp butter
1 onion, chopped
¾ tsp hot gluten-free curry
   powder*

*3 hard-cooked eggs, chopped
15ml/1 tbsp lemon juice
3 tbsp chopped fresh parsley
salt and freshly ground black
   pepper*

Poach the fish in enough water to cover for 10 minutes or until cooked. Drain and reserve the liquid. Remove and discard the skin and bones. Flake the fish and set aside.

Boil the rice in the reserved cooking liquid, adding water if necessary to make up the required quantity.

Melt 60g/4 tbsp of the butter in a large saucepan. Gently sauté the onion until soft but not brown. Stir in the curry powder and cook, stirring, for 1 minute. Add the rice, flaked fish, hard-cooked eggs, lemon juice, parsley and remaining butter. Season to taste. Warm through gently. Turn on to a warmed serving dish.

MEAT

Country pâté

Serves 12

Each serving: 150Cals/630kJ, 0 g fiber

115g/5 slices bacon
675g/1½ lb calves' liver
225g/½ lb chicken livers
1 egg, beaten

30ml/2 tbsp heavy cream
10ml/2 tsp brandy
1 clove garlic, crushed
*salt and freshly ground black
  pepper*

Preheat the oven to 325°F/170°C.

Line a 1kg/9×5×3-in loaf pan with the bacon. Grind together the two kinds of liver and add the egg, cream, brandy and garlic. Season to taste. Mix well. Spoon the mixture into the loaf pan and smooth the top. Cover with foil. Place the pan in a dish with enough water to come halfway up the sides. Bake for about 2 hours. The pâté is cooked when it begins to come away from the sides of the pan. Leave to cool. Cover with a plate or waxed paper, put a weight on top and chill overnight. Just before serving, turn the pâté out of the pan.

Korma gosht (meat curry)

Each serving: 290Cals/1220kJ, 0 g fiber

30ml/2 tbsp vegetable oil
1 onion, sliced
2 bay leaves
1 cinnamon stick
8 peppercorns
8 cloves
4 cardamoms

*450g/1 lb lamb or stewing beef,
  cubed*
4 cloves garlic, crushed
*15g/2 tbsp fresh ginger root, peeled
  and finely chopped or 1 tsp
  ground ginger*
1 tsp chili powder
1 tsp ground turmeric

1 tsp ground cumin
1 tsp ground coriander
140ml/²/₃ cup plain yogurt

salt
chopped fresh coriander leaves or
  parsley

Heat the oil in a large pan and sauté the onion until light brown. Add the bay leaves, cinnamon, peppercorns, cloves and cardamoms and continue cooking for 30 seconds. Add the meat, stir in the garlic and the remaining spices and cook, stirring, for about 7 minutes. Stir in the yogurt, add 285ml/1¼ cups of water, cover and cook over a gentle heat for 40 minutes. Add salt to taste. Garnish with coriander leaves or parsley. Serve with plain boiled rice and cucumber raita (see page 44).

Beef casserole

Each serving: 410Cals/1720kJ, 5 g fiber

30ml/2 tbsp olive oil
450g/1 lb chuck steak, cut into
  cubes
225g/2 cups onion, sliced
1 heaping tbsp gluten-free flour
15g/1 tbsp soy bran
285ml/1¼ cups red wine or dry
  cider
1 clove garlic, chopped

2 sprigs fresh thyme or ½ tsp dried
  thyme
1 bay leaf
salt and freshly ground black
  pepper
115g/1¾ cups field mushrooms,
  sliced
115g/5 slices smoked bacon, cut
  into cubes

Preheat the oven to 275°F/140°C.
    Heat half the olive oil in a large heavy-based casserole. Add the cubes of beef and sauté to seal on all sides. Remove them as they brown and set aside on a plate. Brown the onion in the casserole. Return the meat, stir in the flour and bran and pour in the wine or cider, stirring well. Add the garlic, herbs and seasoning and bring to a boil. Cover the casserole, place in the oven and cook for 2 hours. Sauté the mushrooms and bacon in the rest of the oil and add to the casserole. Cook for an additional hour.

Meat fondue

A meat fondue can be prepared in the usual way – see any standard recipe book. If bread is to be included as well you will of course use gluten-free bread. The following sauces are all gluten-free and suitable for both beef and lamb fondue: Sauce Tartare, Fresh Tomato, Barbecue, Spanish and Curry sauces (see pages 121–2).

Steak and kidney pudding

Serves 8

Each serving: 430Cals/1810kJ, 4 g fiber

Crust:
225g/2 cups gluten-free flour
1/2 tsp salt
115g/1 cup gluten-free shredded
suet
Filling:
225g/1/2 lb kidney

675g/1 1/2 lb stewing beef, trimmed
and cubed
2 tbsp seasoned gluten-free flour
1 medium-sized onion, chopped
8 large mushrooms, trimmed
30g/1/4 cup soy bran
dash Worcestershire sauce

First make the crust. Mix the flour, salt and suet together and slowly add sufficient water to make a soft dough. Roll out on a board dusted with gluten-free flour and line a 1-quart plain mold, reserving enough to make a lid.

To make the filling, toss the meat in the seasoned flour and place it with the onion, mushrooms and bran into the prepared pastry mold. Add the Worcestershire sauce and enough water to three-quarters fill the mold. Moisten the edges of the crust, put on the pastry lid and seal well. Cover with buttered foil, pleated to allow the pudding to rise, and tie around the neck of the mold with string. Stand the mold on an inverted saucer in a large saucepan. Pour in enough water to reach halfway up the mold. Bring to a boil, cover the pan and simmer for at least 4 hours, adding more water as necessary.

To serve, remove the mold from the saucepan, take off the foil and wrap in a clean cloth. Serve from the mold with a spoon.

Liver and bacon hotpot

Each serving: 450Cals/1890kJ, 4 g fiber

450g/1 lb liver, sliced 0.5cm/1/4-in
thick
2 tbsp gluten-free flour
115g/5 slices bacon, chopped
1 medium-sized carrot, roughly
chopped
1 stalk celery, roughly chopped
60g/1/2 cup rutabaga, roughly
chopped
2–3 large onions, sliced

1 tsp dried sage
salt and freshly ground black
pepper
gluten-free stock or water
5ml/1 tsp Worcestershire sauce
900g/2 lb potatoes, peeled and
sliced
30g/2 tbsp butter, melted

Preheat the oven to 325°F/170°C.

Dredge the liver slices in the flour and place in a shallow casserole. Sprinkle in the remaining flour. Add the bacon and prepared vegetables (except the potatoes) together with the sage and season with salt and pepper. Pour in enough stock or water just to cover. Add the Worcestershire sauce. Cover with a thick layer of potatoes, overlapping the slices. Cover the casserole and bake for 2 hours. Remove the lid and cook for an additional 30 minutes. Brush the potatoes with the butter and brown under a hot broiler.

Meat loaf

See photograph, page 57

Serves 6

Each serving: 290Cals/1220kJ, 1 g fiber

2 large slices gluten-free white or brown bread
45ml/3 tbsp milk
450g/1 lb lean ground beef
225g/½ lb ground pork or gluten-free sausage meat
2 medium-sized onions, minced
1 small green pepper, minced

1 large clove garlic, crushed
15ml/1 tbsp tomato paste
salt and freshly ground black pepper
1 tsp mixed herbs
2 tbsp chopped fresh parsley
1 egg, beaten

Preheat the oven to 375°F/190°C.

Remove the bread crusts and soak the bread in the milk. Squeeze out excess milk. In a large bowl, mix the meats, onions, pepper, garlic and tomato paste thoroughly together and season with salt and pepper. Add the soaked bread, mixed herbs and parsley and mix again. Bind together with the beaten egg. Press the mixture into a 1kg/9×5×3-in loaf pan and bake for 1¼ hours or until cooked. The meat loaf is cooked when it comes away from the sides of the pan. Allow to cool in the pan.

Serve cold, or hot with tomato sauce (see page 121).

Chili con carne

Each serving: 460Cals/1930kJ, 23 g fiber

340g/1½ cups dry red kidney beans, soaked overnight in plenty of cold water
225g/½ lb ground beef
15ml/1 tbsp vegetable oil
2 medium-sized onions, chopped
20ml/4 tsp chili powder
1 tbsp vinegar

1 tsp sugar
30ml/2 tbsp gluten-free tomato paste
140ml/⅔ gluten-free stock
400g/1¾ cups canned tomatoes
1 medium-sized green pepper, seeded and chopped

Drain the beans and discard the liquid. In a large heavy saucepan, sauté the meat in the oil, until browned. Add the onions and sauté for a few minutes until soft. Stir in the drained beans. Blend the chili powder, vinegar, sugar and tomato paste together and add. Pour in the stock and the tomatoes together with their juice. Season to taste and stir to mix well. Bring to a boil, partially cover and boil for 10 minutes, then reduce the heat and simmer gently for 1¼–1½ hours, stirring occasionally, until the beans are tender. Add the green pepper 10 minutes before the end of cooking.

Pork in cider

Each serving: 500Cals/2100kJ, 3 g fiber

15ml/1tbsp vegetable oil
4 pork chops, trimmed
6 slices bacon
salt and freshly ground black
  pepper
5 juniper berries, crushed

2 cloves garlic, crushed
1 large cooking apple, pared, cored
  and sliced
2 medium-sized onions, thinly
  sliced
140ml/²/₃ cup cider
675g/1½ lb potatoes, sliced
a little butter

Preheat the oven to 275°F/140°C.
  Heat the oil in a skillet and sauté the pork to brown on both sides. Remove and place in a shallow casserole. Lightly sauté the bacon and, using a slotted spoon, place on top of the pork. Season to taste: do not oversalt. Spread the juniper berries and garlic on top of the bacon and cover with the apple and onion. Pour on the cider and finish with a layer of overlapping potatoes. Dot with butter, cover with foil and a tightly-fitting lid and bake for 3 hours. Place the dish, uncovered, under a preheated broiler to brown the potatoes. Serve immediately.

Stuffed peppers See photograph, page 57

Each serving: 280Cals/1180kJ, 4 g fiber

2 cloves garlic, finely chopped
2 medium-sized onions, chopped
15ml/1 tbsp olive oil
340g/2½ cups cooked lamb or beef
  cut into small pieces
2 tbsp currants
salt and freshly ground black
  pepper

½ tsp ground cinnamon
½ tsp marjoram
400g/1¾ cups canned tomatoes
4 red or green peppers
225g/1 cup long-grain white or
  brown rice, cooked
20ml/4 tsp gluten-free tomato paste

Preheat the oven to 375°F/190°C.
  Sauté the garlic and onions in the olive oil in a skillet for a few minutes, then add the meat and the currants. Season, add the cinnamon, marjoram and two of the tomatoes and 15ml/1 table-spoonful of their juice. Leave, uncovered, to simmer very gently.

Meanwhile, cut off the stalk ends of the peppers and pull out the core and seeds. Rinse under cold water to remove all the seeds. Stand upright in a small casserole. Add the cooked rice to the meat mixture and mix thoroughly. Check seasoning. Fill the peppers with as much of the mixture as you can and put any remaining around the bases of the peppers. Top each with 5ml/1 teaspoonful tomato paste and pour the rest of the canned tomatoes around the peppers. Cover the casserole and bake for 45–50 minutes or until the peppers are tender.

Lamb stew with dumplings

Each serving of stew: 450Cals/1930 kJ, 5 g fiber

8 dumplings, each: 130Cals/550kJ, 1 g fiber

1 kg/2 lb lean stewing lamb
5 tbsp seasoned gluten-free flour
340g/3 cups onions, sliced
225g/2 cups carrots, sliced
2 medium-sized leeks, sliced
2 large potatoes, sliced
salt and freshly ground black
  pepper
2 tbsp chopped fresh parsley or
  mixed herbs

Dumplings:
85g/3/4 cup all-purpose gluten-free
  flour
1 tsp gluten-free baking powder
1/4 tsp salt
15g/1/2 cup soy bran
30g/2 tbsp margarine
2 tbsp chopped fresh parsley or
  mixed herbs

Trim the meat, remove any excess fat and cut into cubes. Coat in seasoned flour. Put a layer of meat in a large saucepan followed by a layer of onion, carrot, leek and potato; season each layer with salt and pepper. Continue with the layers until everything is used. Add 1.1l/5 cups hot water, bring to a boil, skim off the froth, cover tightly and simmer gently for about 2 hours.

Fifteen minutes before the end of cooking time, make the dumplings. Sift the gluten-free flour, baking powder and salt into a bowl. Mix in the bran. Rub in the margarine, add the herbs and mix to a soft dough with 60–75ml/4–5 tablespoonfuls cold water. With floured hands divide the dough into eight balls.

Transfer the meat and vegetables to a heated serving dish and keep warm. Taste the liquid in the pan and adjust the seasoning. Bring to a boil and add more water or stock, if necessary. Drop in the dumplings, cover and simmer for about 15 minutes.

Arrange the dumplings around the meat and vegetables on the serving dish, pour over some of the liquid and serve immediately.

Meat loaf (*top*, see page 54); Lamb stew with dumplings (*center*);
Stuffed peppers (*bottom*, see page 55)
OVERLEAF: Smoked fish pâté (*top left*, see page 49); Baked stuffed mackerel (*center right*, see page 49); Fish cakes (*left*, see page 50)

Chicken with mushrooms and lima beans

Each serving: 330Cals/1390kJ, 10 g fiber

170g/1 cup dry lima beans
30ml/2 tbsp vegetable oil
1 small onion, finely chopped
115g/1½ cups button mushrooms,
* sliced*
½ small green pepper, sliced
½ small red pepper, sliced
225g/1½ cups cooked chicken, cut
* into small pieces*

45ml/3 tbsp sherry
30ml/2 tbsp light cream
salt and freshly ground black
* pepper*
1 quantity white sauce (see page
* 120)*
chopped fresh parsley

Soak the lima beans overnight in plenty of cold water. Drain, add fresh water to cover, bring to the boil, reduce the heat, cover and simmer for 2 hours or until tender. Add more water during the cooking if necessary.

Heat the oil in a large saucepan and gently sauté the onion, mushrooms and peppers until soft but not brown. Add the chicken into to the pan. Pour in the sherry and the cream and season. Bring to a boil, partially cover and simmer for 3 minutes. Drain the cooked lima beans and add to the chicken mixture. Make the white sauce and stir it into the chicken mixture. Reheat and garnish with chopped parsley. Serve with plain boiled rice.

VEGETARIAN DISHES

Lima bean casserole

Each serving: 290Cals/1220kJ, 13 g fiber

225g/1¼ cups dry lima beans,
* soaked in plenty of cold water*
* overnight*
400g/1¾ cups canned tomatoes
1 small onion, chopped

½ green pepper, chopped
salt and freshly ground black
* pepper*
60g/½ cup Cheddar cheese, grated

Preheat the oven to 350°F/180°C.

Drain the beans and put them into a casserole with the tomatoes, onion and green pepper. Season to taste. Cover and cook for about 2 hours or until the beans are tender. Uncover the casserole, sprinkle the cheese over the top, and cook for a further 15 minutes.

Pancakes (*top,* see page 67); Pizza (*center,* see page 66); Zucchini and red pepper quiche (*bottom,* see page 65)

Mediterranean baked zucchini

Serves 8

Each serving: 210Cals/880kJ, 2 g fiber

1 onion, chopped
45ml/3 tbsp olive oil
3 red or green peppers, seeded and diced
2 cloves garlic, crushed
8 zucchini, trimmed

salt and freshly ground black pepper
lemon juice
170g/1½ cups Cheddar cheese, grated
60g/2oz-can anchovy fillets

Preheat the oven to 400°F/200°C. Butter a baking dish.

In a skillet, sauté the onion gently in the oil until soft but not brown. Add the chopped peppers and garlic and cook for an additional 10 minutes. Bring a large pan of salted water to a boil and cook the zucchini for 8 minutes. Drain the zucchini, allow to cool, and cut in half lengthwise. Using a teaspoon, scoop out a channel about 1cm/½-in deep along each half zucchini. Chop this flesh, add to the pepper mixture and cook for a few more minutes. Put the zucchini shells in the baking dish and season with salt and pepper and a squeeze of lemon juice. Fill each shell with the pepper mixture; top with grated cheese and a strip of anchovy fillet. Bake for 30 minutes or until browned. Serve hot.

Lentil roast

Each serving: 460Cals/1930kJ, 9 g fiber

225g/1⅛ cups dry red or brown lentils, washed (soak brown lentils overnight)
1 large onion, chopped
60g/4 tbsp margarine
3 tomatoes, skinned and chopped

60g/¾ cup cornflakes, crushed
115g/1 cup Cheddar cheese, grated
salt and freshly ground black pepper
mixed herbs, chopped parsley or celery salt, to taste

Preheat the oven to 350°F/180°C. Grease a 1-quart ovenproof dish.

Drain the lentils. Put them in a saucepan with 285ml/1¼ cups water and bring to a boil. Cover the pan, reduce the heat to low and simmer, stirring occasionally, until the lentils are soft and the water is absorbed. Add more water if necessary.

Meanwhile, in a skillet, sauté the onion in the margarine over low heat for about 10 minutes or until soft but not brown. Add the tomatoes and cook for 5 minutes. Mash the lentils, add the cornflakes (reserving a few for the top), the onion mixture and the remaining ingredients. Adjust seasoning. Turn into the greased dish. Sprinkle with the reserved cornflakes and a little more grated cheese if desired. Bake for 30 minutes.

Baked potatoes

Choose large even-sized Idaho potatoes, scrub them and prick several times with a fork. Bake in a hot oven, 400°F/200°C for 1 hour or longer. When done they should be soft when squeezed. Cut open lengthwise and serve with a knob of butter, salt and freshly ground black pepper or one or more of the following fillings (quantities for 4 potatoes):

	Each potato, with filling:
115g/1 cup Cheddar cheese, grated	250Cals/1050kJ, 3 g fiber
200g/8 slices bacon, chopped and broiled	350Cals/1470kJ, 3 g fiber
200g/7oz can tuna, with 15ml/ 1 tbsp chopped fresh parsley	230Cals/970kJ, 3 g fiber
115g/½ cup ham, diced, with 200g/1 cup corn kernels	210Cals/880kJ, 5 g fiber

Vegetable curry

Each serving: 150Cals/630kJ, 8 g fiber

15ml/1 tbsp vegetable oil
1 medium-sized onion, sliced
½ tsp ground ginger
1½ tsp turmeric
¼–1 tsp chili powder, according to how hot you like curry
½ tsp ground coriander
2 tsp salt
freshly ground black pepper
400g/1¾ cups canned tomatoes
1 apple, cored, and sliced
handful mixed dried fruit (e.g., currants and golden seedless raisins)
1 medium-sized potato, peeled and sliced

a selection of vegetables, e.g.,
340g/3 cups green beans, stringed and sliced
2 medium-sized carrots, peeled and sliced
170g/1¾ cups cauliflower florets
115g/1 scant cup zucchini, sliced
115g/1 scant cup squash and cut into cubes

15ml/1 tbsp lemon juice
1½ tsp gluten-free garam masala

Heat the oil in a large saucepan. Gently sauté the onions and ginger for about 10 minutes. Stir in the turmeric, chili, coriander, salt and freshly ground black pepper. Add the tomatoes with their juice, the apple, dried fruit and remaining vegetables. Bring to a boil, cover and simmer until all the vegetables are tender. Stir in the lemon juice and garam masala. Continue to simmer with the lid off so that the sauce can thicken a little.

Serve with plain boiled rice and cucumber raita (see page 44).

Vegetarian pilau

Each serving: 430Cals/1810kJ, 7 g fiber

15ml/1 tbsp vegetable oil
225g/1 cup long-grain rice
4 stalks celery, sliced
3 medium-sized onions, sliced
2 cloves garlic
½ tsp turmeric
60g/⅓ cup dried fruit, e.g.,
* currants or golden seedless*
* raisins*
115g/1¾ cups mushrooms,
* roughly chopped*

115g/¾ cup red or green peppers,
* chopped*
1½ tsp gluten-free yeast extract,
* e.g., Marmite*
15ml/1 tbsp lemon juice
freshly ground black pepper
115g/¾ cup salted peanuts
alfalfa sprouts to garnish

Heat the oil in a saucepan and sauté the rice gently until transparent. Add the celery, onions, garlic and turmeric. Stir-fry for a few more minutes. Add 550ml/2½ cups water, the dried fruit, mushrooms and peppers. Bring to a boil, stir, cover and simmer for 10–15 minutes or until the rice is tender and the water is absorbed. Stir in the yeast extract, lemon juice, freshly ground black pepper and nuts. Turn into a warmed serving dish and garnish with alfalfa sprouts just before serving.

Savory quiche

A quiche shell can be made using either the shortcrust pastry recipe (see page 93) or the basic brown pastry recipe given here. Three fillings are given but other gluten-free fillings can be used.

Brown pastry quiche shell

Quiche shell: 870Cals/3650kJ, 9 g fiber

30g/1oz solid vegetable shortening
30g/2 tbsp margarine or butter
115g/1 cup gluten-free brown
* bread mix*

pinch salt
1 medium egg

Preheat the oven to 400°F/200°C.
   Rub the shortening and margarine very carefully into the bread mix with the salt, taking care not to let it bind together. Beat the egg and work it in, bringing together to form a soft pastry. Add a few drops of water only if the mixture is too dry or crumbly. Turn out on to a board well-dusted with gluten-free flour. Roll out into a circle approximately 23cm/9-in diameter. Lift carefully on to an 18cm/7-in quiche pan and press firmly against the sides. Fold in the overhanging pastry to form a double edge. Prick the base of the pan

well. Line with foil and weigh down with dried beans or rice. Bake for 10–15 minutes to set the pastry. Remove the foil and beans.

Quiche fillings:

Zucchini and red pepper   See photograph, page 60

Filling, for one quiche: 790Cals/3320kJ, 1 g fiber

30g/2 tbsp margarine or butter
2 small zucchini, thinly sliced
1 small red pepper, thinly sliced
1 large clove garlic, crushed
salt and freshly ground black pepper

60g/½ cup Cheddar cheese, grated
140ml/²/₃ cup milk
1 large egg

Mushroom and cheese

Filling, for one quiche: 650Cals/2730kJ, 3 g fiber

30g/2 tbsp margarine or butter
60–120g/1–2 cups mushrooms, sliced
1 medium-sized onion, thinly sliced
salt and freshly ground black pepper

60g/½ cup Cheddar cheese, grated
140ml/²/₃ cup milk
1 large egg

Preheat the oven to 400°F/200°C.

In a skillet, melt the margarine or butter and sauté the prepared vegetables for about 10 minutes. Season. Turn into the half-baked quiche shell and sprinkle with the cheese. Slightly warm the milk in the skillet and pour on to the beaten egg. Adjust seasoning. Pour this custard over the vegetables, place the quiche in the center of the oven and bake for about 15 minutes or until browned and firm. Serve hot or cold.

Bacon and mushroom

Filling, for one quiche: 640Cals/2690kJ, 3 g fiber

15g/1 tbsp butter
1 slice bacon, chopped
115g/1¾ cups mushrooms, sliced
170ml/¾ cup milk

2 large eggs
salt and freshly ground black pepper
chopped fresh parsley

Preheat the oven to 400°F/200°C.

Melt the butter in a skillet, add the bacon and mushrooms and cook gently for a few minutes. Beat together the milk, eggs and seasoning. Put the mushrooms and bacon into the quiche shell and pour over the egg and milk. Bake for 10 minutes, then reduce the temperature to 350°F/180°C and bake for an additional 20 minutes. Garnish with the chopped parsley. Serve hot or cold.

Spaghetti-cheese in tomato sauce

Each serving: 580Cals/2430kJ, 4 g fiber

115g/¼ lb gluten-free spaghetti
60g/½ cup Cheddar cheese, grated
1 quantity fresh tomato sauce (see page 121)

2 tbsp gluten-free bread crumbs
1 tsp dried mixed herbs
15g/1 tbsp butter
30g/¼ cup Parmesan cheese, grated

Preheat the oven to 375°F/190°C. Grease a deep pie plate.

Cook the pasta according to the manufacturer's instructions. Drain and rinse in cold water. Place half the pasta in the pie plate. Sprinkle with the Cheddar cheese. Cover with the rest of the pasta and pour the sauce over. Sprinkle with the bread crumbs mixed with the herbs. Dot with the butter and sprinkle the Parmesan cheese on top. Bake uncovered for about 30 minutes or until the top is crisp and golden.

Freeze before the baking stage. Thaw before baking.

Pizza

See photograph, page 60

Makes 6 slices

Each slice: 420Cals/1760kJ, 2 g fiber

1 recipe basic white scone mix using 225g/2 cups gluten-free flour and omitting the sugar (see page 73)

Topping:
1 medium-sized onion, chopped
15ml/1 tbsp vegetable oil

3 fresh (or canned) tomatoes, skinned and chopped
pinch sugar
salt and freshly ground black pepper
½ tsp oregano
115g/1 cup grated cheese
60g/1 scant cup mushrooms, sliced

Preheat the oven to 400°F/200°C. Sauté the chopped onion in the oil for 7–10 minutes. Add the tomatoes and cook for 5 minutes more. Add the sugar, salt, pepper and oregano to taste. Set aside to cool.

Meanwhile, pat the scone mixture into an 18–20cm/7–8-in circle. Place on a greased ovenproof plate or baking sheet.

When the topping is cool spread on top of the base. Put the cheese on top and decorate with slices of mushroom. Put the pizza in the oven and bake for 20 minutes. Reduce the heat to 375°F/190°C and bake for an additional 10–15 minutes. Freezes well.

For a change use a brown scone base (see page 73).

Yorkshire pudding

Makes 8 individual puddings

Each pudding: 100Cals/420kJ, 0 g fiber

*115g/4oz self-rising gluten-free
    flour
pinch salt
1 egg*

*285ml/1¼ cups milk and water
    (half and half)
30g/2 tbsp beef dripping or bacon
    fat*

Preheat the oven to 425°F/220°C.

Place the flour and salt in a mixing bowl: make a well in the center with a wooden spoon. Drop the egg and half the milk and water into it. Gradually work the flour into the egg and milk to form a smooth batter. Slowly add the rest of the milk and water and beat well. Heat the fat in 8–10 muffin cups or in a 23×18cm/9×7-in tin, in the oven. When the fat begins to smoke, pour in the batter. Bake in the top of the oven until well-risen and brown (about 20 minutes for the small puddings or 45 minutes for the large pudding). Serve immediately.

Pancakes

See photograph, page 60

Makes 4 small pancakes

Each pancake: 120Cals/500kJ, 0 g fiber

*30ml/2 tbsp all-purpose gluten-free
    flour
pinch salt
1 medium egg*

*90ml/6 tbsp milk
20ml/4 tsp vegetable oil*

Sift the flour and salt together into a bowl. Make a well in the center, drop in the egg and 15ml/1 tablespoonful of the milk. Beat with a wooden spoon until smooth. Continue beating for 2–3 minutes. Beat in the rest of the milk. Leave to stand for at least 5 minutes. Alternatively, combine all the ingredients in a blender.

Heat the oil in a 15cm/6-in heavy skillet and when very hot pour it off into a cup. Remove the pan from the heat, stir the batter and pour a quarter of it into the skillet. Replace the pan on the heat and cook quickly. When the edge begins to curl, turn the pancake and cook the other side. Turn out on to a hot plate and keep warm. Repeat with the rest of the batter, reheating the oil in the pan and pouring it out before cooking the next pancake.

Fillings

Sweet: squeeze lemon juice on to each pancake, sprinkle with 2 teaspoons sugar and roll up.

Savory: fill each pancake with 2 tablespoonfuls of any hot savory filling, e.g., vegetables in a thick cheese sauce or ground leftover meat or chicken in a mushroom sauce (see white sauce, page 120). Place the rolled-up pancakes in an ovenproof dish, cover with more sauce, sprinkle with grated cheese and reheat in the oven at 400°F/200°C for 15 minutes.

BREADS AND TEABREADS

Gluten gives structure to bread and when gluten-free flour is used bread tends to be more crumbly and cake-like. There are a variety of flours and bread mixes available. It is best to use the type of flour stated in the recipe (self-rising or all-purpose). The leavening agents used are yeast or gluten-free baking powder. Yeast can be bought fresh from bakers or health food stores or dry from grocers and supermarkets. Fresh yeast will keep up to three days in a loosely tied plastic bag in a cool place, and up to a week in a refrigerator. It can be frozen but the maximum storage time will depend on the freshness of the yeast and the storage conditions before it is frozen. The yeast should be weighed out in 15g/2 scant tbsp or 30g/4 scant tbsp cubes and wrapped individually in plastic wrap with a date label. The storage time will be four to six weeks in a freezer. Dry yeast will keep for six months if stored in a tightly sealed container in a cool place. An alternative is active dry yeast, which can be added straight into the flour mix.

Fifteen grams/2 scant tbsp dry yeast is equivalent to 30g/4 scant tbsp fresh yeast. Yeast mixtures rise best if the moisture is kept in. This may be done by covering the container with a sheet of lightly greased plastic wrap or slipping the container into a lightly greased plastic bag during rising.

The time the dough takes to rise in the container varies with the temperature – about 45 minutes in a warm place – a little over an hour at room temperature. Do not over-raise yeast mixtures or they will collapse on baking.

To test if bread is baked, turn it out of the pan and tap the bottom of the loaf – it should sound hollow. Gluten-free bread goes stale quickly, and if you are making it in bulk you should freeze it immediately after baking and cooling. Do not store bread in the refrigerator

Brown bread (*left*, see page 72); White bread (*center*, see page 71); White scones (*above right*, see page 73); Brown scones (*below right*, see page 73)

as this accelerates drying out. Slice loaves before freezing so you can defrost just as much as you need. Put the loaf in a plastic bag and seal, excluding as much air as possible. Many people find that gluten-free bread is better toasted and you can toast it straight from the freezer.

Gluten-free bread will keep well in a freezer for up to six months. Thaw at room temperature for three to four hours or in a refrigerator overnight. Refresh in a hot oven for 5 minutes. Stale bread can be toasted or made into bread crumbs and stored in an airtight container.

See also Baking and breadmaking, page 32, and Which flour to use? page 38.

Gluten-free baking powder

85g/³⁄₄ cup cornstarch
100g/7 tbsp baking soda
60g/4 tbsp cream of tartar
60g/4 tbsp tartaric acid (from the
pharmacy)

Mix all the ingredients together and pass through a fine sieve two or three times. Store in an airtight container in a dry place.

White bread   See photograph, page 69

Makes 2 small loaves

Each loaf: 910Cals/3820kJ, 0 g fiber

430ml/1³⁄₄ cups milk and water
(half and half)
2 tsp dry yeast or 30g/4 scant tbsp
fresh yeast

1 tsp granulated sugar
340g/3 cups all-purpose gluten-free
flour
1 tsp salt
30g/2 tbsp lard

Grease two 0.5kg/8½×4½×2½-in loaf pans. Warm the milk and water until just comfortable to the touch. Put one-third of the milk and water in a bowl, sprinkle the dry yeast on to it and add a pinch of sugar; or, cream the fresh yeast with a pinch of sugar and a little of the warm liquid. In either case, leave to stand in a warm place for about 10 minutes until frothy.

Sift the flour and the salt, add the rest of the sugar and rub in the fat. Make a well in the center and add the yeast and sufficient liquid to make a stiff batter. Beat, adding more milk and water as it thickens

---

Date and walnut loaf (*top left*, see page 75); Banana bran bread (*top right*, see page 74); Butter cob (*bottom*, see page 74)

until you have a smooth batter that drops heavily from the spoon, adding more water, if necessary. Divide the batter between the two pans, cover with oiled waxed paper, or a damp cloth, and set in a warm place for 20–30 minutes or until risen to the top of the pans.

Preheat the oven to 425°F/220°C. Stand the pans on a baking sheet and bake for about 30 minutes, until well risen, firm and a light brown. Cool for a few minutes in the pan and turn on to a wire rack.

Slice and freeze if not to be used at once.

To make one large loaf use a 1 kg/ 9×5×3-in pan, allow 40–50 minutes and reduce the temperature to 400°F/200°C for the last 10 minutes.

Brown bread

See photograph, page 69

Makes 1 small loaf

Each slice: 70Cals/290kJ, 2g fiber

1 tsp dried yeast or 7.5g/1 scant
  tbsp fresh yeast
½ tsp sugar
255ml/1 cup plus 1 tbsp warm
  water at blood heat

225g/2 cups Welplan Baking Mix
½ tsp salt
30g/4 tbsp soy bran

Grease a 0.5kg/8½×4½×2½-in loaf pan.

Dissolve the yeast and the sugar in approximately one-third of the warm water. Leave in a warm place until frothy – about 10 minutes.

Sift together the flour and salt and stir in the soy bran. Add the dissolved yeast and the rest of the water. Beat either by hand (2–3 minutes) or with an electric mixer on slow speed (1–2 minutes) until a thick smooth batter is formed. Put the batter in the loaf pan, cover with oiled waxed paper and stand in a warm place until the top of the batter is level with the top of the pan (normally 30–40 minutes).

Preheat the oven to 450°F/230°C. Bake on a middle shelf for 25–35 minutes or until firm. Let the bread stand in the pan for 5 minutes before removing.

To make 12 rolls, use the above recipe but add only 140–225ml/ ⅔–1 cup water – to make a soft dough.

White scones

See photograph, page 69

Makes 8

Each scone: 210Cals/880kJ, 1 g fiber

*225g/2 cups self-rising gluten-free
  flour*
1/2 tsp salt
1 tsp gluten-free baking powder
60g/4 tbsp margarine, chilled

60g/4 tbsp granulated sugar
*60g/1/3 cup mixed dried fruit
  (optional)*
approximately 140ml/2/3 cup milk

Preheat the oven to 400°F/200°C. Grease a baking sheet.
    Sift flour, salt and baking powder into a bowl. Add the margarine cut into pieces and rub in until the mixture resembles bread crumbs. Add the sugar, and fruit if used and mix to a soft dough with the milk. Roll out on a board dusted with gluten-free flour to about 1cm/1/2-in thick and cut into circles with a plain cookie cutter. Or divide into two, shape into circles 1cm/1/2-in thick and mark into four. Place on the baking sheet and bake 10–15 minutes for small scones or 20–25 minutes for the larger scones. They should be well risen and browned. Cool on a wire rack.

Brown scones

See photograph, page 69

Makes 8

Each scone: 120Cals/500kJ, 4 g fiber

*280g/2½ cups Welplan Baking
  Mix*
½ tbsp gluten-free baking powder
1 tsp salt
45g/6 tbsp soy bran

60g/4 tbsp margarine, chilled
1 tbsp sugar
170–225ml/3/4–1 cup milk

Preheat the oven to 400°F/200°C. Grease a baking sheet.
    Sift the flour, baking powder and salt together into a bowl. Add the soy bran. Rub in the margarine until the mixture resembles bread crumbs. Add the sugar. Mix to a sticky dough with the milk. Roll out on a board dusted with gluten-free flour to about 1cm/ ½-in thick. Cut into rounds with a plain cutter. Place on the baking sheet and bake for 15–20 minutes or until lightly browned. Cool on a wire rack and store in an airtight container.

Alternatives
For cheese scones, omit sugar and add 60–85g/1/3–½ cup grated hard cheese.
    For fruit scones, add 60–85g/1/3–½ cup dried fruit with the sugar.
    For pizza base, omit sugar.

Butter cob

See photograph, page 70

Makes 2 loaves or 16 small rolls

Each roll: 160Cals/670kJ, 0 g fiber

*450g/4 cups all-purpose gluten-free
  flour
pinch salt
2 tsp gluten-free baking powder*

*115g/¼ lb (1 stick) butter
½ tsp sugar
280ml/1⅛ cups milk (or more, as
  required)*

Preheat the oven to 400°F/200°C. Dust a baking sheet with gluten-free flour. Sift the flour and baking powder into a large bowl, rub in the butter and add the sugar. Mix with sufficient milk to make a sticky dough. Knead lightly to bring it together. Form into two large cobs 2–4cm/1–1½-in thick and mark the tops with a cross.

Bake the loaves for 20 minutes and then reduce the heat to 375°F/190°C for 10 minutes covering with aluminum foil if it browns too quickly.

Alternatives   Make into 16 small rolls or a pizza base, using one-third of the amounts for an 18cm/7-in pizza. Bake the rolls for 15 minutes at 400°F/200°C. For the pizza, see page 66.

Corn bread

Makes 16 slices

Each slice: 80Cals/340kJ, 0 g fiber

*115g/1 scant cup cornmeal
115g/1 cup all-purpose gluten-free
  flour
1 tsp salt
1 tbsp gluten-free baking powder*

*1 tbsp brown sugar
200ml/⅞ cup milk
1 medium egg
60g/4 tbsp butter, melted*

Preheat the oven to 425°F/220°C. Grease a 20cm/8-in square pan.

Sift together the cornmeal, flour, salt and baking powder. Stir in the sugar. Beat the egg lightly and add the milk and melted butter. Stir into the dry ingredients, mixing well. Pour the mixture into the pan and bake for 20–30 minutes, until lightly browned. Cool in the pan for 5 minutes and remove to a wire rack.

Banana bran bread

See photograph, page 70

Makes 16 slices

Each slice: 160Cals/670kJ, 4 g fiber

*115g/½ cup soft margarine
115g/¾ cup soft brown sugar*

*1 large egg
2 large ripe bananas, mashed*

225g/2 cups all-purpose gluten-free
   flour
1 tsp gluten-free baking powder
1 tsp gluten-free allspice

85g/½ cup raisins
60g/½ cup soy bran
milk to mix, as necessary

Preheat the oven to 350°F/180°C. Grease a 1 kg/9×5×3-in loaf pan and line the bottom with waxed paper.

Cream the margarine and sugar until light. Beat the egg, mash the bananas and gradually add to the creamed mixture. Sift together the flour, baking powder and allspice, and add the dried fruit, bran and sufficient milk to form a stiff dropping mixture. Spoon into the pan, level the mixture and bake in the center of the oven for 1¼–1½ hours. Leave in the pan for 5 minutes, then remove to a wire rack. Store in a plastic bag in a cool place. Freezes well.

This loaf can be served as a plain cake or sliced and buttered.

Bran fruit loaf

Makes 2 small loaves

Each slice: 60Cals/250kJ, 5g fiber

400g/14oz mixed dried fruit
340ml/1½ cups cold tea
255g/1⅛ cups all-purpose gluten-
   free flour
1 tbsp gluten-free baking powder

¼ tsp gluten-free allspice
115g/1 cup soy bran
70g/½ cup brown sugar
2 large eggs, beaten

Preheat the oven to 350°F/180°C. Grease two 0.5kg/ 8½×4½×2½-in loaf pans well.

Soak the fruit in the tea for at least 30 minutes. Sift together flour, baking powder and allspice. Mix in the soy bran and the sugar. Add the fruit, tea and eggs and beat together well. Divide the mixture between the two loaf pans and bake for 1 hour or until brown and firm. Leave in the tin for a few minutes and then turn out on to a wire rack.

Date and walnut loaf   See photograph, page 70

Makes 16 slices

Each slice: 190Cals/800kJ, 1 g fiber

225g/1½ cups chopped dates
170g/1 cup dark brown sugar
85g/6 tbsp margarine
grated rind of 1 orange
30ml/2 tbsp orange juice

1 medium egg
225g/2 cups all-purpose gluten-
   free flour
1½ tsp gluten-free baking
   powder
1 tsp ground cinnamon
60g/½ cup chopped walnuts

Preheat the oven to 350°F/180°C. Grease a 1 kg/9×5×3-in loaf pan and line the bottom with greased waxed paper.

Simmer the dates with 140ml/²/₃ cup water in a covered pan for 15 minutes or until soft. The water should all be absorbed by the time the dates are cooked; if it tends to dry out add more. Stir in the sugar and margarine and remove pan from the heat. Add the grated orange rind and juice, beat in the egg. Sift the flour, baking powder and cinnamon together and add to the mixture. Add the walnuts. Mix well and spoon into the prepared pan. Bake for 1 hour 10 minutes–1 hour 20 minutes, until a skewer comes out clean. Cool in the pan for 5 minutes, then remove to a wire rack. Store wrapped in foil in a cool place. Serve sliced as it is, or buttered.

Canadian muffins

See photograph, page 79

Makes 6

Each muffin: 130Cals/550kJ, 0 g fiber

1 medium egg
60ml/¼ cup milk
15ml/1 tbsp melted butter
115g/1 cup all-purpose gluten-free
  flour

pinch salt
1½ tsp gluten-free baking powder
1 tbsp granulated sugar

Preheat the oven to 400°F/200°C. Grease six muffin pan cups.

Beat the egg and milk in a bowl. Add the melted butter, and stir well. Sift the gluten-free flour, salt and gluten-free baking powder together and stir in the sugar. Add the egg mixture to the dry ingredients, stirring only just enough to mix. *Do not beat* and do not mix until smooth; the batter should be coarse and stiff. Place 2 heaping teaspoonfuls in each cup. Bake for 20 minutes or until well-risen and brown.

Best served warm immediately after cooking. If the muffins are left to go cold, they can be rewarmed by being wrapped loosely in aluminum foil and heated in a hot oven (450°F/230°C) for 5 minutes.

Alternatives   For savory or sweet muffins add the following:
60g/¹/₃ cup crisp cooked bacon,
  crumbled (omit sugar)
60g/½ cup grated cheese (omit
  sugar)
60g/½ cup chopped nuts
60g/¹/₃ cup any dried fruit

These should be mixed with the dry ingredients.

Russian pancakes (blini)

See photograph, page 79

Makes 20

Each pancake: 40Cals/170kJ, 0 g fiber

115g/1 cup buckwheat flour
45g/6 tbsp Welplan Bread Mix
with Added Soya Bran
1 tsp gluten-free baking powder

½ tsp baking soda
¼ tsp salt
1 tsp sugar
340ml/1½ cups buttermilk or milk
soured with 5ml/1 tsp vinegar

Grease a griddle or heavy skillet. Sift the buckwheat into a bowl with the bread mix, baking powder, baking soda and salt – tip in any grains that remain in the sieve. Add the sugar. Add the buttermilk or soured milk to the dry ingredients, stirring to combine. Do not beat. This forms a very thin batter. Leave to stand for a few minutes.

Warm the griddle over a medium heat. Drop tablespoons of the batter carefully on to the griddle, leaving room for them to spread. They will form about 7cm/3-in pancakes. Cook for 2–3 minutes until bubbles appear on the surface. They will lift easily with a spatula. Turn and cook for 2–3 minutes more. Regrease the griddle or pan between additions as necessary. Pile on to a dish and keep warm. Serve at once.

These go well with breakfast dishes such as bacon, sausages, scrambled eggs. They are equally good with honey, maple syrup or jam.

Welsh griddle cakes

See photograph, page 79

Makes 12

Each cake: 150Cals/630kJ, 1 g fiber

vegetable oil to grease the griddle
225g/2 cups all-purpose gluten-free
flour
pinch salt
1½ tsp gluten-free baking powder
¼ tsp grated nutmeg or gluten-
free allspice (optional)

85g/6 tbsp margarine
60g/4 tbsp granulated sugar
60g/⅓ cup currants
1 large egg
a little milk to mix
superfine sugar to dust

Grease and heat a griddle or heavy skillet to a moderate heat. Sift the gluten-free flour, salt and gluten-free baking powder and spice, if using, into a bowl. Rub in the margarine, add the sugar and currants. Beat the egg, add about a tablespoonful of milk, pour on to the dry mixture and bring together. Work into a stiff paste, adding more milk if necessary. Turn out on to a board dusted with gluten-free flour and pat or roll into a circle, not less than 0.5cm/¼-in thick.

Cut into triangles or circles with a cookie cutter. Lift with a spatula on to the hot griddle. Cook each side for 4–5 minutes or until set, adjusting the heat as necessary. When cooked lift on to a piece of waxed paper and dust with sugar on both sides.

Serve immediately or buttered when cold.

DESSERTS

As well as the recipes in this section, sago and tapioca are gluten-free, and fruit is an easy and healthy way to end a meal. Ready-made pie fillings, dessert mixes and ice creams may contain gluten (see also the table on page 28).

COLD DESSERTS

Muesli

Each serving (dry): 180Cals/760kJ, 7 g fiber

60g/³/₄ cup rolled oats (see page 30)   *30g/¹/₄ cup chopped walnuts*
2 tbsp soy bran   *30g/¹/₃ cup stoned dates*
2 tbsp sunflower seeds   *30g/¹/₄ cup raisins*

Mix all the ingredients together. They may be mixed in a large quantity and stored in a screw-top jar. Grated eating apple or fresh or stewed fruit in season may be added, and the muesli sweetened with honey or brown sugar. Muesli can be eaten alone or with milk or gluten-free yogurt. For those who cannot tolerate oats, substitute another tablespoon of soy bran and more sunflower seeds and add some flaked coconut.

Muesli can also be eaten as a snack, or for breakfast.

Canadian muffins (*top left*, see page 76); Blinis (*center*, see page 77); Welsh griddle cakes (*bottom*, see page 77)
OVERLEAF: Baked lemon delight (*top left*, see page 89); Fruit crumble (*bottom left*, see page 87); Apple Brown Betty (*right*, see page 88)

Pineapple cheesecake

Makes 12 slices

Each slice: 210Cals/880kJ, 0 g fiber

Base:
9 gluten-free cookies
60g/4 tbsp butter
30g/3 tbsp light brown sugar
a little ground cinnamon (optional)

Top:
15g/2 tbsp unflavored gelatin
115ml/½ cup pineapple juice

170g/2 slices pineapple cut into
pieces
2 large eggs, separated
85g/6 tbsp superfine sugar
225g/1 8oz package cream cheese
or 1 cup sieved cottage cheese
140ml/²/₃ cup sour or heavy cream
angelica to decorate

Grease an 18–20cm/7–8-in loose-bottomed cake pan.

To make the base, crush the crackers. Melt the butter and mix with the sugar, cinnamon and cookie crumbs. Press the mixture on to the base of the pan and leave in a cool place to set.

Meanwhile, put the gelatin and the pineapple juice in a cup. Stand the cup in a pan of barely simmering water and stir until the gelatin has dissolved. Leave to cool. In a mixing bowl, beat the egg yolks and sugar until light and thick. Add the dissolved gelatin, the cheese and the cream. Beat again and stir in the pineapple pieces, reserving a few for decoration. Finally, when it is on the point of setting, fold in the stiffly beaten egg whites. Pour on to the prepared base and leave to set in the refrigerator (about 2–3 hours). Remove from the pan and slide the cake on to a serving plate. Decorate with the reserved pineapple and angelica.

Alternatives Lemon or orange cheesecake: use the grated rind and juice of two lemons or two oranges in place of the pineapple pieces and the pineapple juice.

Strawberries or raspberries (115g/¾ cup) can be used as a topping for a lemon cheesecake.

Sponge tart base

Makes 8 slices

Each slice: 80Cals/340kJ, 0 g fiber

2 large eggs
60g/¼ cup superfine sugar

70g/²/₃ cup all-purpose gluten-free
flour

Preheat the oven to 400°F/200°C. Grease a tart pan 20cm/8-in in diameter and place on a baking sheet.

Fruit sherbert (*top and center left*, see page 85); Pineapple cheese-cake (*center right*); Fruit and nut iced pudding (*bottom*, see page 85)

Whisk the eggs and sugar together until thick and light. The mixture must leave a trail from the whisk which remains for a few seconds. Sift the flour on to the mixture and fold in very lightly with a metal spoon. Finally, fold in 15ml/1 tablespoonful of boiling water. Do not mix or beat any further. Pour the batter into the pan and bake for 15 minutes. The sponge should be firm, golden brown and springy to the touch. Leave to cool in the pan for at least 5 minutes. Ease out carefully and cool on a wire rack with the top side down.

Suggested fillings When cool, fill with seasonal fresh fruit such as strawberries or raspberries, or any drained canned fruit. If using fresh fruit, stew a few berries in about 140ml/²/₃ cup water to extract the flavor. Drain the juice and measure it. Take 200ml/⅞ cup of juice; blend a tablespoonful of cornstarch with a little of the juice and bring the rest to a boil. Pour on to the cornstarch, return to the pan and boil for 5 minutes, until it coats the back of a spoon. Sweeten to taste. Pour over the tart. If using canned fruit, use the juice in the same way, but it may not need any extra sugar.

Lemon meringue pie

Serves 6

Each serving: 330Cals/1390kJ, 0 g fiber

Pastry shell:
125g/1 cup gluten-free flour
pinch salt
60g/4 tbsp margarine or butter,
  chilled
1 medium egg, beaten

Filling:
30g/¼ cup cornstarch
grated rind and juice of 2 lemons
115g/½ cup granulated sugar
2 large eggs, separated

Preheat the oven to 400°F/200°C. Make the pastry (see shortcrust pastry, page 93), roll it out on a surface dusted with gluten-free flour and line a quiche pan or deep pie plate 18cm/7-in in diameter. Prick the pastry all over with a fork. Line with foil and weight down the foil with dried beans or rice. Bake the pastry shell for 15 minutes. Remove the foil and beans or rice and bake for a further 5 minutes to brown. Remove the pastry shell from the oven and reduce the temperature to 300°F/150°C.

Meanwhile prepare the filling. Blend the cornstarch, lemon rind and juice, and 140ml/²/₃ cup water in a saucepan. Bring to a boil, stirring all the time, then simmer for a few minutes. Remove from the heat and add all but 2 tablespoonfuls of the sugar. Beat the egg yolks into the mixture. Pour into the pastry shell. Whip the egg whites stiffly and fold in the 2 tablespoonfuls of sugar. Pile the meringue on top of the pie, covering the filling completely. Place in the cool oven for 15–20 minutes to set and brown lightly. Serve warm or cold. Do not freeze.

Fruit sherbert
See photograph, page 82

Each serving: 150Cals/630kJ, 8 g fiber

450g/1 lb berries
115g/½ cup granulated sugar
285ml/1¼ cups water

5ml/1 tsp unflavored gelatin
2 large egg whites

Turn the refrigerator to the coldest setting or turn on the fast-freeze section of the freezer.

Purée the fruit and sieve if necessary to remove seeds. In a saucepan, dissolve the sugar in the water and bring to a boil. Boil rapidly for 5 minutes and set aside to cool. Sprinkle the gelatin over a little water in a pan and when soaked heat gently to dissolve. Then mix together the syrup, purée and gelatin and put into a suitable container. Freeze until just mushy, about 30 minutes. Stir to remove ice crystals around the edges. Whisk the egg whites until stiff and fold into the purée. Return to the freezer for at least 2 hours. To serve allow to defrost for 10–15 minutes – the exact time will depend on the temperature of your freezer and the fruit used.

Serve with gluten-free Danish cookies if liked (see page 99).

Raspberry mousse

Each serving: 240Cals/1010kJ, 5 g fiber

425g/16-oz can raspberries
170g/1 package (6-oz) raspberry gelatin dessert

170g/¾ cup evaporated milk
5ml/1 tsp lemon juice

Strain the raspberries and measure the juice. Prepare the gelatin dessert according to package directions, using the juice from the raspberries in place of some of the water. Leave to cool and refrigerate until it is beginning to set. Purée the raspberries. Place the evaporated milk and lemon juice in a bowl and whisk until the mixture is very thick and will hold soft peaks. Fold in the raspberry purée and the gelatin mixture. Pour into a serving bowl and leave to set, preferably in a refrigerator.

Other fruit and a complementary flavored gelatin can be used.

Fruit and nut iced pudding
See photograph, page 82

Serves 12

Each serving: 170Cals/710kJ, 1 g fiber

115g/¾ cup mixed dried fruit
60g/4 tbsp maraschino cherries or 17 washed candied cherries, quartered

30ml/2 tbsp sherry
200ml/⅞ cup milk
1 tsp unflavored gelatin
1 tsp powdered instant coffee

1 tsp gluten-free cocoa
60g/½ cup chopped walnuts
60g/¼ cup superfine sugar

a few drops vanilla extract
285ml/1¼ cups whipping cream
chopped nuts and cherries for
decoration

Turn refrigerator to lowest setting or switch on the fast-freeze section of a freezer.

Mix the fruits and the sherry and leave to stand for about 30 minutes. Warm the milk and dissolve the gelatin in it. Add the coffee and cocoa. Remove from the heat and cool in a large bowl. When cold add the soaked fruit and sherry, nuts, sugar and vanilla extract. Whip the cream until it forms soft peaks, fold into the fruit mixture and turn into a bowl. Freeze for about 1 hour. Take out of the freezer and mix well with a fork to distribute the fruit evenly. Re-freeze until required.

Remove from freezer about 30 minutes before serving. Dip the bowl into hot water for a second and turn on to a serving dish. Sprinkle with the nuts and cherries.

Dutch fruit salad

Each serving: 180Cals/760kJ, 4 g fiber

225g/8oz can pineapple chunks
60g/¼ cup sugar (optional)
rind of 1 lemon
juice of ½ lemon
340g/2½–3 cups fresh fruit, e.g.,
  apples, plums, oranges,

melon, grapes and berries
15–30ml/1–2 tbsp kirsch
chopped preserved ginger
(optional)

Drain the pineapple, saving the juice. Make the juice up to 285ml/1¼ cups with water or orange juice. Place in a small saucepan with the sugar. Add the lemon rind and juice. Heat gently, stirring to dissolve the sugar. Bring to a boil and simmer for 5 minutes. Leave to infuse for 20 minutes. Meanwhile prepare the fruits, cutting them into suitable sized pieces (if using bananas, slice into the salad just before serving). Pour the cooled syrup over the fruit. Stir in the kirsch, and pieces of ginger, if using. Chill in the refrigerator.

Simple ice cream

Each serving: 340Cals/1430kJ, 0 g fiber

285ml/1¼ cups milk
2 tbsp gluten-free custard powder
115g/½ cup superfine sugar
285ml/1¼ cups heavy cream, well
  chilled, or 400g/1¾ cups

evaporated milk, well chilled
a few drops vanilla extract
(optional)

Turn the refrigerator to its lowest setting or switch on the fast-freeze section of a freezer.

Make a custard with the milk and custard powder as directed on the package. Add the sugar. Set aside to cool. Whip the cream or evaporated milk until very thick. Add the cold custard and mix well. Flavor if desired with vanilla extract. Pour into freezing trays and freeze until just set around the sides. Return to a bowl and whisk. Replace in the freezing trays and freeze until hard. Store in a deep freezer. Remove from the freezer 30 minutes before required and keep in the refrigerator until served.

May be flavored by adding instant coffee or other gluten-free flavorings to the milk during the making of the custard.

HOT DESSERTS

Baked custard

Each serving: 170Cals/710kJ, 0 g fiber

2 eggs
30g/2 tbsp granulated sugar
550ml/2½ cups milk

a few drops vanilla extract
*   (optional)*
grated nutmeg

Preheat the oven to 325°F/170°C. Grease a 1 l/1 quart ovenproof dish.

Beat the eggs lightly with the sugar. Warm the milk to blood heat and pour on to the eggs and sugar. Mix well, adding vanilla extract, if using. Pour the custard into the pie dish. Grate a little nutmeg on top. Place the dish in a pan of water in the oven; the water should come about halfway up the sides of the dish – this prevents the custard curdling. Bake for 1 hour or until the custard sets. Serve warm or cold.

Baked apples go well with this and can be baked at the same time.

Fruit crumble   See photograph, page 80

Serves 6

Each serving: 360Cals/1510kJ, 6 g fiber

450g/1 lb raw fruit, e.g., plums,
*   cooking apples, gooseberries or*
*   rhubarb*
115g/²/₃ cup brown sugar,
*   according to taste; some fruits*
*   need more than others*

30g/4 tbsp soy bran
85g/6 tbsp margarine, chilled
60g/½ cup walnuts or toasted
*   filberts, finely chopped (optional)*
30g/3 tbsp dark brown sugar

Topping:
140g/1¼ cups gluten-free flour

Preheat the oven to 350°F/180°C. Grease a 1l/1 quart ovenproof dish.

Prepare the fruit, mix with the brown sugar and place in the ovenproof dish. Mix the gluten-free flour and soy bran and rub in the margarine until the mixture resembles fine bread crumbs. Stir in the nuts, if using, and dark brown sugar. Sprinkle over the fruit and press gently down. Place in the center of the oven. Bake for about 1 hour, until the fruit is tender. If the top browns too quickly reduce the heat to 325°F/170°C. Serve hot with gluten-free custard or cold with cream.

Alternatives   A little dried fruit or chopped ginger may be added to the raw fruit, and allspice or cinnamon to the brown sugar.

Apple brown Betty

See photograph, page 81

Each serving: 440Cals/1850kJ, 4 g fiber

60g/4 tbsp butter
8 gluten-free cookies, crushed, or
  85g/7/8 cup dry gluten-free
  bread crumbs
140g/3/4 cup brown sugar

450g/1 lb cooking apples
juice of 1 lemon
1 tsp ground cinnamon
1/4 tsp ground nutmeg
grated rind of 1/2 lemon

Preheat the oven to 350°F/180°C. Grease a 1.5 l/1½ quart oven-proof dish.

Melt the butter and add the bread or cookie crumbs and 30g/3 tbsp of the brown sugar. Mix well. Line the bottom of the dish with a third of this mixture. Peel, core and slice the apples very thinly and put in a bowl. Sprinkle with the lemon juice, and mix in the remaining brown sugar, spices, lemon rind and 30ml/2 tablespoonfuls of water. Stir well. Place half this mixture on top of the crumbs in the dish. Cover with a further third of the crumbs, repeat the fruit layer and top with the remainder of the crumbs. Press down lightly. Cover with greased waxed paper and bake in the center of the oven for about 40 minutes or until the apples are nearly soft. Increase the heat to 400°F/200°C, remove the waxed paper and cook for 15 minutes more until the top is crisp and brown.

An alternative   Add a tablespoonful of dried mixed fruit to each layer of apples.

Old-fashioned rice dessert

Each serving: 240Cals/1010kJ, 3 g fiber (bran included)

700ml/3 cups milk
60g/1/4 cup short-grain rice
15g/2 tbsp soy bran (optional)
45g/3 tbsp granulated sugar

2 pieces lemon rind
15g/3 tbsp butter
1/2 tsp grated nutmeg

Preheat the oven to 325°F/170°C. Grease a 1 l/1 quart ovenproof dish.

Warm the milk. Put the rice, bran, if using, sugar, lemon rind and butter in the dish and pour the milk over. Stir to dissolve the sugar. Add the nutmeg and stir again. Bake for 2–3 hours, stirring once or twice during the first hour, and then leave undisturbed for the remaining time.

Baked lemon delight
See photograph, page 80

Each serving: 280Cals/1180kJ, 0 g fiber

60g/4 tbsp soft margarine
60g/4 tbsp granulated sugar
2 medium eggs, separated

1 tbsp gluten-free flour
grated rind and juice of 1 large
lemon
285ml/1¼ cups milk

Preheat the oven to 350°F/180°C. Grease a 1 l/1 quart ovenproof or soufflé dish.

Cream the margarine and sugar together until very light. Beat in the egg yolks and then the flour, lemon rind and juice. Beat well. Mix in the milk carefully, do not worry if it curdles a little. Beat the egg whites until they just hold peaks and fold in carefully. Pour into the greased dish and bake for 45 minutes. It should be slightly risen and firm on top. Serve hot or cold.

Orange dessert

Each serving: 320Cals/1340kJ, 0 g fiber

60g/4 tbsp soft margarine
60g/4 tbsp superfine sugar
1 large egg
grated rind of 1 orange
85g/¾ cup all-purpose gluten-free
flour

pinch salt
¼ tsp gluten-free baking powder
15–30ml/1–2 tbsp milk
3 tbsp orange marmalade
(optional)

Grease a 0.5 l/2½ cup plain mold. In a mixing bowl, cream the margarine and sugar until light. Beat in the egg and orange rind. Sift together the gluten-free flour, salt and gluten-free baking powder and fold into the creamed mixture. Add milk as required to form a soft dropping consistency. Spread the marmalade, if using, on the bottom of the mold and spoon in the mixture. Cover first with greased waxed paper, and then with foil, folding and twisting it over the rim of the mold to keep out the steam. Place in a steamer or in a covered pan containing water halfway up the sides of the mold. Bring to a boil and steam for 50–60 minutes. Carefully add more boiling water as necessary. Serve hot with gluten-free custard or marmalade sauce.

Bread pudding

Each serving: 550Cals/2310kJ, 2 g fiber

60g/4 tbsp butter or margarine
6 slices gluten-free bread
4 tbsp thick marmalade (optional)
1 medium-sized cooking apple,
  grated or thinly sliced

85g/1/2 cup brown sugar
60g/1/3 cup raisins
1 tsp ground cinnamon (optional)
2 large eggs
430ml/13/4 cups milk

Preheat the oven to 350°F/180°C. Grease a 1.5 l/1½ quart oven-proof dish.

Butter each slice of bread and spread with marmalade, if using. Make a layer of the bread and marmalade in the bottom of the dish. Cover with half the apple, half the sugar and half the raisins, and some cinnamon, if using. Repeat once and end with a layer of bread and marmalade, buttered side down. Dot with a little more butter and a sprinkling of sugar. Beat the eggs and milk together and pour over. Press down and leave to stand at least 30 minutes. Bake for about 45 minutes or until the custard is set and the top is crispy. Serve hot or cold.

English Christmas pudding

Each serving: 270Cals/1130kJ, 3 g fiber

30g/4 tbsp all-purpose gluten-free
  flour
pinch salt
1/4 tsp gluten-free allspice
pinch baking soda
grated rind of 1/2 lemon
60g/1/2 cup cooking apple, grated
60g/1/3 cup brown sugar
30g/1/4 cup chopped almonds
60g/1/3 cup golden seedless raisins

60g/1/3 cup currants
30g/3 tbsp raisins
30g/3 tbsp chopped mixed peel
45g/1/3 cup gluten-free shredded
  suet
70g/2/3 cup dry gluten-free bread
  crumbs
1 large egg
45–60 ml/3–4 tbsp milk

Grease a 0.5kg/3 cup plain mold. Sift the flour, salt, allspice and baking soda into a large mixing bowl. Add the lemon rind, apple, sugar, almonds, dried fruit, shredded suet and bread crumbs. Mix well. Beat the egg with the milk. Gradually stir into the mixture, which should form a soft dropping consistency: if it is too stiff add a little more milk. Spoon into the mold, cover with greased waxed paper and then with foil. Place in a steamer or in a covered pan containing water halfway up the sides of the mold. Bring to a boil

---

Profiteroles (*top*, see page 96); Almond fruit pastries (*center*, see page 94); Brandy snaps (*bottom*, see page 104)

and steam for 5 hours, adding boiling water as necessary. Allow to cool. Cover with new foil or a cloth and seal well.

When ready for use, steam for 1–1½ hours and serve.

This dessert improves with keeping and can be stored for up to a year. If it becomes dry, moisten with a little cider or milk before re-steaming.

PASTRIES, COOKIES AND SMALL CAKES

Gluten-free pastry is very good. If it cracks when it is being rolled out it is because it is too dry. Always add a few teaspoonfuls more water than you think necessary. Do not roll out too thinly: it should be about 0.5cm/¼-in thick or more. If you are not going to use the pastry immediately, wrap it in a plastic bag or foil to prevent it drying out, and store in a refrigerator or freezer.

See also Baking and breadmaking, page 32, and Which flour to use? page 38.

Shortcrust pastry

Sufficient for 12 small tarts or 1 x 18cm/7-in single pie crust

115g/4 oz pastry: 950Cals/3990kJ, 0 g fiber

115g/1 cup all-purpose gluten-free flour
pinch salt
30g/2 tbsp solid vegetable shortening or lard (from the refrigerator)

30g/2 tbsps margarine, chilled
1 medium egg

Preheat the oven to 400°F/200°C.

Sift the flour and salt into a bowl. Cut the shortening and margarine

Coconut squares (*top and center left*, see page 106); Plain oatmeal biscuits (*top right and bottom left*, see page 100); Danish cookies (*center right*, see page 99); Nutty squares (*bottom right*, see page 102)

into the flour and then, using your fingertips, rub in lightly until the mixture resembles dry bread crumbs. Beat the egg with 15ml/1 tablespoonful cold water. Sprinkle it over the crumb mixture and mix lightly. This should form a pliable but not sticky dough. If you are not using the pastry immediately, make a wetter dough as it tends to dry out on standing. To roll out, lightly dust a board and a rolling pin with gluten-free flour, place the dough on the board and roll firmly, lifting and flouring underneath to prevent sticking. Do not roll less than 0.5cm/¼-in thick. Use as required.

Note: There is no need to grease pans or dishes when using short-crust pastry. It will not stick if you use at least half the quantity of fat to flour. Prick well before filling to prevent the pastry rising. You will need pastry made with 170g flour for a 2-crust tart 18cm/7-in diameter.

Rich sweet crust pastry

Sufficient for 24 small tarts or 2×18cm/7-in single pie crusts

225g/8oz pastry: 1930Cals/8110kJ, 0 g fiber

225g/2 cups all-purpose gluten-free flour
pinch salt
115g/¼ lb (1 stick) butter or margarine, chilled

60g/4 tbsp superfine sugar
1 large egg
5–10ml/1–2 tsp lemon juice

There is no need to grease the pans to be used.
   Sift the flour and salt into a bowl. Cut the butter into small pieces and rub into the flour until the mixture resembles fine bread crumbs. Stir in the sugar. Beat the egg with the lemon juice and sprinkle over the crumb mixture. Bring together gently and knead into a ball. Add a few drops of water if the pastry is too dry. It should form a soft pliable dough. Preheat the oven to 400°F/200°C. Wrap the pastry in foil and chill for 30 minutes in the refrigerator. Do not roll out less than 0.5cm/¼-in thick. Use as required.

Almond fruit pastries   See photograph, page 91

Makes 6 wedges

Each wedge: 220Cals/920kJ, 2 g fiber

60g/4 tbsp soft margarine
60g/¼ cup ground rice (see page 38)
60g/½ cup all-purpose gluten-free flour
1 large eating apple, unpared

60g/6 tbsp plus a little extra soft brown sugar
30g/¼ cup ground almonds
slivered almonds to decorate

Preheat the oven to 425°F/220°C. Grease an ovenproof dish or pan 20cm/8-in in diameter.

Blend the margarine, ground rice and flour together with a fork. Grate half the apple and mix it in with 60g/6 tbsp of the sugar and the ground almonds. Knead into a ball. Press out on the pan. Thinly slice the rest of the apple and arrange in circles on the pastry, working towards the center. Sprinkle with a little more sugar and decorate with the slivered almonds. Bake for 20 minutes, or until browned. Cut into wedges and serve warm or cold.

For variety, mix some cinnamon with the brown sugar sprinkled on the top.

Welsh cheese cakes

Makes 12

Each cake: 230Cals/970kJ, 0 g fiber

½ recipe rich sweet crust pastry
  (see opposite)

Filling:
raspberry jam
45g/3 tbsp soft margarine
45g/3 tbspsuperfine sugar

1 medium egg
30g/4 tbsp all-purpose gluten-free
  flour
60g/¼ cup ground rice (see page
  38)
½ tsp gluten-free baking powder
confectioner's sugar

Preheat the oven to 400°F/200°C.

Roll and cut out the pastry into 6cm/2½-in circles. Line twelve tartlet pans with the pastry and place a small teaspoonful of jam in each. In a bowl, cream the margarine and sugar until very light and beat in the egg. Sift together the flour, ground rice and baking powder. Fold into the creamed mixture with the vanilla extract. Divide equally among the twelve tarts. Bake for 15 minutes, then reduce the heat to 375°F/190°C for an additional 5 minutes. Cool on a wire rack. Dust with confectioner's sugar to serve.

Apple cinnamon shortbread

Makes 12 pieces

Each piece: 150Cals/630kJ, 2 g fiber

150g/1¼ cups all-purpose gluten-
  free flour
1 tsp gluten-free baking powder
½ tsp cinnamon
30g/4 tbsp soy bran
85g/6 tbsp margarine or butter,
  chilled

85g/6 tbsp plus 1 tbsp superfine
  sugar
1 medium egg, beaten
170g/1½ cups cooking apples,
  pared, cored and thinly sliced

Preheat the oven to 350°F/180°C. Grease an 18cm/7-in square or a 20cm/8-in round pan and line with waxed paper. Sift the flour, baking powder and cinnamon together into a bowl. Mix in the bran, and rub in the margarine or butter. Stir in 85g/6 tbsp of the superfine sugar. Work most of the egg into the mixture and knead until smooth, adding more egg if the pastry is too dry to roll out. Divide the pastry in half and roll out one half to fit the pan. Line the base of the pan with the pastry. Place the sliced apples over the pastry and press down. Roll out the other half of the pastry and place over the apple. Press down well and brush with a little milk. Mark with a fork and sprinkle with the extra tablespoon of sugar. Bake for 30–40 minutes or until lightly browned. Leave to cool in the pan. Lift out, peel off the paper and cut the shortbread into bars. Will keep for several days, wrapped, in a refrigerator.

An alternative   Substitute 2.5ml/½ teaspoonful ground ginger for the cinnamon and spread a thick layer of ginger marmalade on the pastry in place of the apple.

Mince pies

Makes 12

Each pie: 230Cals/970kJ, 0 g fiber

*1 recipe rich sweet crust pastry (see
  page 94)
340g/2 cups gluten-free mincemeat*

*egg white or milk to glaze
confectioner's sugar*

Preheat the oven to 400°F/200°C.
   Roll out the pastry, cut out twelve circles using a 6cm/2½-in pastry cutter and line twelve tartlet pans. Cut out lids using a cutter one size smaller. Fill with the gluten-free mincemeat. Moisten the edges with water and cover with the lids, pressing the edges well down to seal. Make a slit in each pastry to let out the steam. Brush the tops with egg white or milk. Bake for 15–20 minutes or until golden brown. Cool on a wire rack and dust with confectioner's sugar before serving.

Choux pastry for profiteroles or chocolate éclairs
See photograph, page 91

Makes 15 éclairs or puffs

Each: 140Cals/590kJ, 0 g fiber

*85g/¾ cup all-purpose gluten-free
  flour
pinch salt
45g/3 tbsp margarine, chilled
2 medium eggs
140ml/²/₃ cup heavy or whipping
  cream, whipped until stiff*

Chocolate candied icing:
*10ml/2 tsp gluten-free cocoa
170g/1½ cups confectioner's sugar*

Chocolate sauce:

45g/1½ squares semisweet gluten-free baking chocolate, broken into pieces
5ml/1 tsp cornstarch

pinch salt
60g/4 tbsp granulated sugar
15g/1 tbsp butter

Preheat the oven to 425°F/220°C. Grease a large baking sheet. Sift the flour and salt together. Put 140ml/⅝ cup water and the margarine into a small saucepan over high heat. When the margarine has melted, bring to a boil. Add the flour all at once, remove pan from the heat and beat until smooth. Beat one egg in until the mixture is smooth and glossy. Repeat with the second egg. It should form a stiff paste. For profiteroles, place teaspoonfuls on the baking sheet. For éclairs, pipe 7cm/3-in lengths, using a 2cm/1-in nozzle. Bake for 25–30 minutes in the middle of the oven. Do not open the door for at least 25 minutes. When the puffs are well risen, browned and crisp remove from the oven. Cut a slit in each to allow the steam to escape and leave to cool on a wire rack. When cold fill with whipped cream. Cover with chocolate candied icing. Alternatively, the filled puffs may be piled on a dish and chocolate sauce poured over them.

To make the icing, dissolve the cocoa in a little warm water (15–30ml/1–2 tablespoonfuls) and gradually add to the confectioner's sugar. The icing should be thick enough to coat the back of a spoon: if needed add water or sugar to adjust. Use at once.

To make the chocolate sauce, add 115ml/½ cup water to the chocolate in a small saucepan and melt over a low heat. Mix the cornstarch and salt with a little water to make a smooth paste. Bring 85ml/6 tbsp water to a boil and pour on to the blended cornstarch, stirring. Return to the pan and bring back to a boil, stirring continuously. Add the chocolate and the sugar and cook for 4–5 minutes, stirring and beating. Finally, stir in the vanilla extract and the butter, leave to cool and pour over the puffs.

Shortbread

Makes 15 bars

Each bar: 110Cals/460kJ, 0 g fiber

140g/1¼ cups all-purpose gluten-free flour
30g/2 tbsp ground rice (see page 38)
60g/4 tbsp granulated sugar plus a little for dusting

115g/¼ lb (1 stick) butter (not straight from the refrigerator, but not soft)

Preheat the oven to 350°F/180°C.

Mix the flour and ground rice in a large bowl and stir in the sugar. Place the butter in one piece in the bowl and work in with one hand, kneading until the mixture binds together and becomes smooth. Turn on to a board dusted with gluten-free flour and shape into a rectangle.

Roll out into a strip 30×7cm/12×3-in and about 1cm/½-in thick. Nip the edges between thumb and forefinger as you go along to form a pattern. Prick well and dust with a little granulated sugar. Cut into strips 1.5–2cm/¾–1-in wide. Use a spatula to place well apart on an ungreased baking sheet and bake in the middle of the oven for 20–30 minutes or until pale golden. Cool on the baking sheet. Store in an airtight container when cool.

Basic cookie mix

Makes 36 cookies

Each cookie: 70Cals/290kJ, 1 g fiber

170g/1½ cups gluten-free flour　　*170g/¾ cup superfine sugar*
60g/½ cup soy bran　　　　　　　*1 large egg*
115g/½ cup soft margarine　　　　*milk to mix, as necessary*

any of the following may be added to the mixture:
30–60g/¼–½ cup chopped nuts, candied peel, ginger pieces, chopped candied cherries, grated orange or lemon rind, or gluten-free chocolate chips

Preheat the oven to 375°F/190°C. Grease two or three baking sheets.
　Sift flour into a bowl and add the other ingredients. Work together with a wooden spoon and then knead lightly to form a ball. Add a little milk if the dough will not hold together. Turn on to a board dusted with gluten-free flour and roll into a sausage not more than 30cm/12-in long. Wrap it in waxed paper and refrigerate for 30 minutes. When firm cut into 0.5cm/¼-in slices with a sharp knife and lift on to a baking sheet, leaving space for the slices to spread. Bake for 15–20 minutes, until well browned. Cool on a wire rack. Store in an airtight container. If you wrap the dough in foil it freezes very well.
　May be decorated with glacé icing and an almond or a cherry, or coated with melted gluten-free chocolate.

Cheese crackers

Makes 20

Each cracker: 40Cals/170kJ, 0 g fiber

60g/½ cup well-flavored cheese,　　*pinch cayenne pepper (optional)*
*　grated*　　　　　　　　　　　　*½ tsp salt*
85g/¾ cup all-purpose gluten-free　*60g/4 tbsp margarine or butter,*
*　flour*　　　　　　　　　　　　　*　chilled*

Grease a baking sheet.
　Mix the cheese, flour, cayenne pepper, if using, and salt in a bowl

and rub the fat in. Dust your hand with gluten-free flour and knead mixture into a ball. Wrap the dough in plastic wrap or waxed paper and refrigerate for 30 minutes. Preheat the oven to 375°F/190°C. Roll out on to a board dusted with gluten-free flour to 0.5cm/¼-in thick. Prick well and cut into small circles. Put the crackers on the baking sheet and bake for 10–15 minutes until pale gold – do not overcook or the cheese may become bitter. Cool on a wire rack and store in an airtight container.

Crisp crystal cookies

Makes 20

Each cookie: 90Cals/380kJ, 2 g fiber

140g/1¼ cups all-purpose gluten-free flour
60g/¼ cup ground rice (see page 38)
85g/6 tbsp superfine sugar
60g/½ cup soy bran

115g/¼ lb (1 stick) butter or margarine, chilled
1 medium egg, separated
a little light brown sugar

Preheat the oven to 350°F/180°C. Grease two baking sheets.

Mix the flour, ground rice, sugar and bran. Rub in the butter or margarine until the mixture resembles fine bread crumbs. Add the egg yolk and knead until smooth. Wrap the dough in waxed paper and refrigerate for 30 minutes. Roll out to 0.5cm/¼-in thickness. Use a 7cm/3-in cookie cutter to cut out the cookies and place them well apart on the prepared sheet. Brush the cookies with the lightly beaten egg white and sprinkle with dark brown sugar. Bake for 15 minutes or until golden brown. Leave to cool a little and then remove to a wire rack. Store in an airtight container.

For variety add a little cinnamon to the sugar before sprinkling it over the cookies.

Danish cookies

See photograph, page 92

Makes 30

Each cookie: 100Cals/420kJ, 2 g fiber

225g/2 cups all-purpose gluten-free flour
60g/½ cup soy bran
170g/¾ cup (1½ sticks) slightly salted butter
115g/½ cup granulated sugar
60g/½ cup chopped almonds

2–3 drops almond extract
1 medium egg yolk, beaten
1 egg white, lightly beaten
a little granulated sugar
30 slivered almonds

Preheat the oven to 350°F/180°C. Grease two baking sheets.

Mix the flour and bran and lightly rub in the butter. It will be difficult so do not try to form "fine bread crumbs", just break it up. Add the sugar, almonds and extract and rub again to mix evenly.

Bind together with the egg yolk. Turn on to a board lightly dusted with gluten-free flour. Form into a sausage and work into a smooth roll, not more than 30cm/12-in long. Wrap in waxed paper and chill in the refrigerator until firm, at least 30 minutes. Roll into walnut-sized balls, press flat and place well apart on the baking sheets. Brush with the lightly beaten egg white and sprinkle a little sugar on each. Decorate with a slivered almond. Bake until golden brown, about 20 minutes. Leave on the baking sheets for 5 minutes to set. Cool on a wire rack and store in an airtight container.

New Zealand cookies

Makes 30

Each cookie: 90Cals/380kJ, 1 g fiber

140g/²/₃ cup softened margarine or butter
1 tbsp golden syrup – measure with a warmed spoon
60g/¹/₃ cup brown sugar
115g/1 cup 4oz self-rising gluten-free flour

115g/1¹/₂ cups rolled oats (see page 30)
1 tsp ground ginger, or to taste
60g/³/₄ cup flaked coconut
¹/₂ tsp baking soda

Preheat the oven to 325°F/170°C. Grease two baking sheets. Slowly melt the margarine or butter, golden syrup and sugar in a large pan. Remove from the heat. Mix together the flour, oats, ginger and coconut. Dissolve the baking soda in 15ml/1 tablespoonful hot water, add to the pan and then add the dry ingredients. Cool for 10–15 minutes or until the mixture becomes stiff. Take walnut-sized pieces and pat into balls in your hands. Place on the prepared sheets, flatten slightly, leaving room for them to spread a little. Bake for 20–30 minutes, or until golden brown. Cool on a wire rack. The cookies keep well stored in an airtight container.

Plain oatmeal biscuits   See photograph, page 92

Makes 24

Each biscuit: 70Cals/290kJ, 1 g fiber

85g/1 cup rolled oats (see page 30)
115g/1 cup medium oatmeal
85g/³/₄ cup gluten-free flour
¹/₂ tsp salt

60g/4 tbsp margarine, chilled
140ml/²/₃ cup (or as required) milk soured with 1 tsp vinegar

Preheat the oven to 375°F/190°C. Dust one or two baking sheets with gluten-free flour.

Mix the dry ingredients together in a large bowl. Rub in the margarine and mix with sufficient milk to make a soft sticky dough. Place on a board lightly floured with gluten-free flour. Roll out to 0.5cm/¼-in thick. Prick well. Cut into squares with a sharp knife. Place on baking sheets and bake until lightly browned, 15–20 minutes. Remove to a wire rack. Store in an airtight container.

A plain biscuit to eat with cheese or jam. They keep well.

To make a sweet version of this biscuit add 60g/⅓ cup brown sugar.

Oat crunchies

Makes 20

Each cookie: 90Cals/380kJ, 1 g fiber

115g/¼ lb (1 stick) margarine or   *115g/⅔ cup light brown sugar*
butter
130g/1⅛ cups rolled oats (see page
30)

Preheat the oven to 375°F/190°C. Grease a 28×18cm/11×7-in baking pan and line it with greased waxed paper.

Gently melt the margarine or butter, do not allow it to brown. Mix the oats and the sugar in a bowl. Pour the melted fat on to the mixture and mix well. Turn on to the baking sheet and press it down firmly with your hands. Bake in the center of the oven for 15–20 minutes or until pale gold, turning the pan after 10 minutes to insure even baking. Cut into squares whilst still hot. Leave in the pan to cool. When cold store in an airtight container.

Golden bars

Makes 14

Each bar: 150Cals/630kJ, 1 g fiber

115g/⅔ cup soft brown sugar   *15ml/1 tbsp golden syrup –*
115g/¼ lb (1 stick) butter or   *measure with a warmed spoon*
margarine   *¾ tsp ground ginger*
170g/2⅛ cups rolled oats (see page
30)

Preheat the oven to 300°F/150°C. Grease a jelly roll pan (28×18cm/ 11×7-in).

Melt the sugar and butter or margarine in a saucepan. Stir in the oats, syrup and ginger. Press the mixture evenly into the prepared pan. Bake for 40 minutes or until golden brown. Allow to cool slightly and score into bars with a sharp knife.

The cookies may be stored in an airtight container for up to 1 week.

Nutty squares

See photograph, page 92

Makes 24

Each square: 100Cals/420kJ, 1 g fiber

*115g/¼ lb (1 stick) butter or
  margarine
200g/2½ cups rolled oats (see
  page 30)
60g/¹/₃ cup raisins or golden seedless
  raisins*

*60g/¹/₃ cup dark brown sugar
60g/½ cup unsalted chopped
  peanuts
1 medium egg, beaten*

Preheat the oven to 350°F/180°C. Grease 1 28×18cm/11×7-in shallow pan and line with greased waxed paper. Melt the butter or margarine. Mix all the dry ingredients in a large bowl, add the beaten egg and then the melted butter. Mix well. Press firmly into the pan. Bake for 40–45 minutes or until well browned. Score into squares while warm. Cool in the pan. Store in an airtight container.

Ginger snaps

Makes 24 cookies

Each cookie: 90Cals/380kJ, 0 g fiber

*225g/2 cups Welplan Baking Mix
2 tsp gluten-free baking powder
pinch salt
1 tsp ground ginger
115g/½ cup superfine sugar*

*85g/6 tbsp margarine
60ml/4 tbsp golden syrup –
  measure with a warmed spoon
1 medium egg, beaten*

Preheat the oven to 350°F/180°C. Grease two baking sheets.

Sift together the flour, baking powder, salt and ground ginger. Stir in the sugar. Melt the margarine and golden syrup together and add to the dry ingredients with the beaten egg. Mix together well.

Place small teaspoonfuls of the mixture in mounds on the baking sheets.

Bake in the center of the oven for about 15 minutes. Leave to cool slightly, then transfer to a wire rack.

Date-nut squares

Makes 15

Each square: 140Cals/590kJ, 3 g fiber

*85g/6 tbsp margarine
115g/²/₃ cup pitted dates, chopped
60g/¹/₃ cup soft brown sugar
30g/¼ cup walnuts, chopped
30g/2 tbsp candied cherries,
  chopped*

*60g/1⁷/₈ cups Rice Krispies
30g/4 tbsp soy bran
115g/4 squares gluten-free
  semisweet chocolate*

Grease an 18cm/7-in square cake pan and line the bottom with greased waxed paper.

Place the margarine and the dates in a pan and heat slowly. Stir in the sugar and cook for a few minutes. Mix in the walnuts, cherries, Rice Krispies and bran. Press the mixture firmly into the prepared pan. Melt the chocolate in a bowl over hot water, allow to cool slightly and spread over the cookie mixture. Chill in a refrigerator until set. Cut into bars.

Peanut bars

Makes 12

Each cookie: 120Cals/500kJ, 2 g fiber

60g/4 tbsp soft margarine
60g/¹/₃ cup brown sugar
1 medium egg, beaten
¹/₂ tsp gluten-free baking powder
¹/₄ tsp ground cinnamon

85g/³/₄ cup all-purpose gluten-free flour
30g/4 tbsp soy bran
60g/¹/₂ cup gluten-free salted peanuts
milk to mix, as necessary

Preheat the oven to 350°F/180°C. Grease an 18cm/7-in square pan.

Cream the margarine and sugar until light and fluffy. Beat the egg and blend into the creamed mixture. Sift the baking powder, cinnamon and flour together and fold into the mixture. Add the bran, the peanuts and a little milk if the mixture is too dry. Spread in the prepared pan and bake on the middle shelf until well browned, 20–30 minutes. Score into bars and leave to cool. Turn on to a wire rack while still warm. When cold store in an airtight container; they will keep for about a week.

Chocolate nut bars

Makes 24

Each bar: 130Cals/550kJ, 1 g fiber

170g/6 squares semisweet gluten-free chocolate
115g/1 cup walnuts, coarsely chopped
60g/4 tbsp butter or margarine

115g/1¹/₃ cups flaked coconut
85g/6 tbsp superfine sugar
grated rind of ¹/₂ orange
1 egg

Preheat the oven to 350°F/180°C. Grease a jelly roll pan 28×18cm/11×7-in and at least 3cm/1-in deep, and line the base with a strip of waxed paper.

Break the chocolate into pieces and melt in a bowl over a pan of hot water. Stir in the chopped nuts. Spread the chocolate nut mixture evenly over the base of the pan. Leave to cool. Put the remaining ingredients into a bowl and beat until the mixture forms a smooth paste. Spread evenly over the chocolate. Bake for 25 minutes or until golden brown. Leave until cold and then cut into slim bars.

Florentines

Makes 24

Each cookie: 80cals/340kJ, 1 g fiber

60g/4 tbsp butter
60g/4 tbsp granulated sugar
2 tsp whipping cream
30g/2 tbsp candied cherries,
  chopped
30g/¼ cup chopped mixed peel

60g/½ cup almonds, finely
  chopped
60g/½ cup almonds, slivered
115g/4 squares gluten-free
  semisweet chocolate

Preheat the oven to 350°F/180°C. Cover two large baking sheets with non-stick baking paper.

Melt the butter and sugar in a saucepan. Stir in the cream and remove from the heat. Blend in the rest of the ingredients except the chocolate. Place teaspoonfuls of the mixture well apart on the prepared baking sheets. Bake for 10–15 minutes or until golden brown. Melt the chocolate in a bowl over hot water. When the cookies are cold turn them over and spread the underside of each cookie with a teaspoonful of chocolate. Leave to harden and store in an airtight container.

Brandy snaps   See photograph, page 91

Makes 20

Each snap: 90Cals/380kJ, 0 g fiber

30ml/2 tbsp golden syrup –
  measure with a warmed spoon
60g/4 tbsp margarine or butter
60g/4 tbsp granulated sugar
60g/½ cup all-purpose gluten-free
  flour

2.5ml/½ tsp ground ginger
5ml/1 tsp brandy or rum extract
225ml/1 cup whipping cream,
  whipped until stiff

Preheat the oven to 325°F/170°C. Generously grease two baking sheets.

Put the golden syrup, margarine or butter and sugar in a pan and heat gently. Stir until the sugar has dissolved and the butter is melted – do not boil. Sift together the flour and ginger and beat into the syrup until smooth. Stir in the brandy or rum extract. Place 4–6 heaping teaspoonfuls, well spaced, on to each baking sheet. Bake one sheet at a time for 10 minutes each, turning the tray around after 5 minutes to insure even cooking. When the cookies are golden brown, remove the pan and allow to cool for about 30 seconds. When the cookies are just beginning to set, lift them with a spatula and fold over the greased handle of a wooden spoon. Mold around the handle and rest on the baking sheet to cool. Slip the curled brandy snap on to a wire rack. If the cookies set too quickly, return to the oven for a minute or two to soften and try again. After a little practice it is quite simple – using two wooden spoons makes it easier. Fill with whipped cream to serve but store unfilled in an airtight container.

Note: Brandy snaps are difficult to make but can be perfected with practice. This recipe makes excellent very thin, crisp snaps; here are some points to aid success.
- The baking sheets must be very well greased – use butter or oil.
- Measure the ingredients very carefully, especially the syrup if you are making a smaller quantity.
- At first, bake just two snaps at a time for better, quicker removal from the baking tray. As you become more skilled you can bake up to four at a time.

Melting moments
See photograph, page 109

Makes 20

Each cookie: 70Cals/290kJ, 0 g fiber

115g/¼ lb (1 stick) butter or margarine
45g/5 tbsp confectioner's sugar
60g/½ cup self-rising gluten-free flour

60g/½ cup cornstarch
3–4 drops vanilla extract

Preheat the oven to 325°F/170°C. Cover two baking sheets with greased waxed paper or non-stick baking paper.
Cream the margarine or butter with the sugar until very light. Sift the flours together and work into the creamed mixture with the vanilla extract until very smooth. Pipe small cookies on to the prepared pans or, with gluten-free floured hands, form walnut-sized pieces into balls and flatten slightly with the back of a fork. Bake for about 20 minutes until pale gold. Allow to cool on a wire rack. Store in an airtight container.

Alternatives
Sandwich together with a thick butter icing.
Add a few drops of very strong coffee to the mixture and sandwich with the coffee-flavored cream icing.
For Viennese cookies, pipe the mixture in swirls and decorate with a piece of candied cherry.

Coconut squares

See photograph, page 92

Makes 9

Each square: 230Cals/970kJ, 2 g fiber

60g/4 tbsp soft margarine
30g/2 tbsp granulated sugar
1 medium egg
85g/¾ cup all-purpose gluten-free
*   flour*
pinch salt
30g/4 tbsp soy bran

30ml/2 tbsp raspberry jam

Topping:
85g/1 cup flaked coconut
85g/6 tbsp granulated sugar
1 medium egg

Preheat the oven to 350°F/180°C. Grease an 18cm/7-in square pan and line with waxed paper.

Cream the margarine and sugar until light and fluffy. Beat in the egg. Sift the flour and salt together and mix in. Stir in the bran. Spread this mixture over the base of the prepared pan. Warm the jam and spread on top. Mix the topping ingredients in a small bowl, spread on top of the jam, and score the top lightly with a fork. Bake for 30–40 minutes or until lightly browned and firm. Leave to cool in the pan, then cut into squares. Store in a cool place.

Coconut-cherry chocolate slices

Makes 12

Each slice: 210Cals/880kJ, 2 g fiber

85g/6 tbsp soft margarine
60g/4 tbsp granulated sugar
1 large egg
115g/1¹/₃ cups flaked coconut
30g/4 tbsp gluten-free flour

60g/¼ cup candied cherries,
*   chopped*
115g/4 squares semisweet gluten-
*   free chocolate*
15g/1 tbsp butter

Preheat the oven to 350°F/180°C.

Grease an 18cm/7-in square pan and line the bottom with greased waxed paper.

Cream the margarine and sugar until light. Beat in the egg. Mix the flaked coconut with the flour and fold it in. Add the candied cherries. Smooth into the prepared pan and bake for 20–30 minutes or until firm and brown. Leave in the pan to go cold. Melt the chocolate and butter in a small bowl placed over hot water, allow to cool and pour it over the cookies. As the chocolate sets mark wavy lines with a fork and score into bars. Store in a cool place.

Almond macaroons

Makes 15

Each macaroon: 50Cals/210kJ, 1 g fiber

1 egg white
70g/¹/₃ cup superfine sugar

70g/²/₃ cup ground almonds
2 drops almond extract

Preheat the oven to 350F/180°C. Cover a baking sheet with non-stick baking paper.

Whisk the egg white until frothy but not too stiff. Fold in the sugar, ground almonds and extract. Take walnut-sized pieces, roll quickly and lightly into balls (dip hands in cold water if the mixture becomes too sticky). Place on the baking sheet, leaving room for the macaroons to spread. Bake for 20–25 minutes or until pale golden. Allow to cool on the paper. Lift off when cold and store in an airtight container.

One tablespoonful of the ground almonds may be omitted and 1 tablespoonful ground rice used in its place.

Spicy doughnuts

See photograph, page 109

Makes 9

Each doughnut: 350Cals/1470kJ, 0 g fiber

For coating:
115g/¹/₂ cup granulated sugar
1–2 tsp grated nutmeg

1 medium egg
115g/¹/₂ cup granulated sugar
115ml/¹/₂ cup milk

45g/3 tbsp margarine
340g/3 cups all-purpose gluten-free flour
2 tsp gluten-free baking powder
¹/₄ tsp salt
¹/₄ tsp ground cinnamon
¹/₄ tsp ground nutmeg
vegetable oil for sautéing

Put a layer of paper towels on a baking sheet to drain the doughnuts. Mix 115g/½ cup granulated sugar and grated nutmeg on a sheet of waxed paper. A slotted spoon is useful to slip the doughnuts into the oil and lift them out

Beat the egg and whisk in the sugar and the milk. Melt the margarine and beat it in. Sift the dry ingredients together and fold into the egg and milk mixture. Mix to form a soft dough. Knead lightly to form a ball. Wrap in waxed paper and chill for 30 minutes until firm. Press the dough into a piece about 1cm/½-in thick on a board dusted with gluten-free flour. Cut with a 5cm/2-in doughnut cutter. Heat the oil in a deep skillet until hot. Test by dropping in a cube of gluten-free bread, which should brown in 30 seconds. Cook the doughnuts in the hot oil until light brown. Drain and dredge in the sugar and nutmeg. Serve at once.

Chelsea buns

Makes 8

Each bun: 300Cals/1260kJ, 1 g fiber

115ml/⅝ cup milk
½ tsp sugar
1 tsp dry yeast
255g/2¼ cups Welplan Bread Mix
1 tsp ground cinnamon
½ tsp grated nutmeg
30g/2 tbsp margarine

30g/2 tbsp butter
85g/1½ cup currants
30g/2 tbsp sugar

Glacé icing:
170g/1½ cup confectioner's sugar, sifted
2–3 drops vegetable oil

Preheat the oven to 400°F/200°C. Grease a small baking sheet.

Warm the milk to blood heat. Dissolve half a teaspoonful of sugar in the milk and sprinkle the dry yeast on the top. Leave in a warm place to froth for about 10 minutes. Sift the bread mix and spices into a large bowl and rub in the margarine. Add the yeast and milk mixture and bind together with a knife. Knead lightly. Cover with waxed paper and leave in a warm place for about 30 minutes or until doubled in bulk. Turn on to a board dusted with gluten-free flour and roll out to a 25cm/10-in square. Melt the butter and brush it over the dough. Sprinkle with the currants and sugar and roll up firmly like a jelly roll. Moisten the edge with water to seal. Cut into eight slices and place cut side down on the greased baking sheet. Cover again with waxed paper or a damp cloth. Put in a warm place and leave to prove for 20 minutes or until well risen. Bake near the top of the oven for 15 minutes. Reduce the heat to 375°F/190°C for an additional 5–10 minutes. Remove the buns from the oven and cool on a wire rack. Make the candied icing by gently heating 30ml/2 tbsp water in a saucepan. Gradually beat in the confectioner's sugar and oil. The icing should be smooth, glossy and of a pouring consistency, so add a little more water if necessary. When the buns are cool, drizzle a little icing over each.

These buns are best eaten the day they are made, but they do freeze well. Allow them to go cold and then freeze promptly.

Spicy doughnuts (*top left*, see page 107); Coffee-sandwiched melting moments (*top right*, see page 105); Chelsea buns (*bottom*)

CAKES

Cakes baked with gluten-free flour turn out very well, but here are a few points to aid success. Check the cake ten to fifteen minutes before the end of the baking time: if it is browning too quickly, lower the temperature and/or cover it with waxed paper. To test if a fruit cake or teabread is baked, push a skewer or knitting needle into the middle – when it is done the skewer will come out clean. To test a sponge cake, push the center lightly with a finger and it should spring back. Leave all cakes in the pan for at least five minutes after baking and then cool on a wire rack. If a cake cracks during baking it is usually because it is baking too quickly.

Cakes are best frozen straight after baking and cooling. They can be decorated first (take care that the decorations are gluten-free) but keep longer if undecorated. Storage time for decorated cakes is four to six weeks, undecorated cakes about three months. Thaw cakes at room temperature. The thawing time depends on how thick the cake is – one hour for small cakes, two to three hours for larger cakes.

See also Baking and breadmaking, page 32, and Which flour to use? page 38.

Victoria sandwich cake

Makes 10 slices

Each slice: 220Cals/920kJ, 0 g fiber

115g/1/2 cup soft margarine
115g/1/2 cup superfine sugar
2 medium eggs
1/4 tsp vanilla extract (optional)
115g/1 cup all-purpose gluten-free flour

pinch salt
1/2 tsp gluten-free baking powder
a little milk
jam
whipped cream

Preheat the oven to 375°F/190°C. Grease two 18cm/7-in sandwich pans and line the bottoms with greased waxed paper.

Cream the margarine and sugar together, beat in the eggs one at a time, and add the vanilla extract, if using. Sift the flour, salt and baking powder together into a bowl and fold into the creamed mixture, adding a little milk if necessary to make a soft-dropping consistency. Divide the batter between the two pans and bake for about 20 minutes or until golden brown and firm. Cool on a wire rack. Sandwich together with jam and cream.

Ginger ring cake (*top*, see page 116); Victoria sandwich (*center*); Rich fruit cake (*bottom*, see page 119)

Alternatives

Use different flavorings, e.g., orange rind, lemon rind or coffee extract.

Add 60g/¹/₃ cup mixed dried fruit and bake in prepared muffin pans for 15–20 minutes. Makes about 12.

Apple cake

Makes 8 slices

Each slice: 310Cals/1300kJ, 1 g fiber

140g/⁵/₈ cup soft margarine
85g/6 tbsp granulated sugar
1 large egg
200g/1³/₄ cups all-purpose gluten-free flour
½ tsp gluten-free baking powder

Filling:
2 large cooking apples, pared, cored and sliced
1 tsp ground cinnamon
85g/6 tbsp granulated sugar

Preheat the oven to 325°F/170°C. Grease an 18cm/7-in square pan or a 20cm/8-in round pan and line with waxed paper.

Cream the margarine and sugar until light. Beat in the egg. Sift together the flour, salt and baking powder and fold into the mixture. Spread three-quarters into the prepared pan. Cover with the sliced apple, and sprinkle with the cinnamon and sugar. Place teaspoonfuls of the remaining mixture on top. Bake in the center of the oven until the cake is set and the apple is soft, about 1–1½ hours. Sprinkle with confectioner's sugar and serve warm or cold as a dessert.

Almond cake

Makes 12 slices

Each slice: 220Cals/920kJ, 4 g fiber

115g/1 cup blanched almonds
140g/²/₃ cup superfine sugar
3 medium eggs
60g/½ cup all-purpose gluten-free flour

½ tsp gluten-free baking powder
45g/6 tbsp soy bran
85g/6 tbsp butter
15ml/1 tbsp kirsch or Amaretto liqueur (optional)

Preheat the oven to 325°F/170°C. Grease two 18–20cm/7–8-in layer cake pans and line the bottoms with greased waxed paper.

Grind the almonds finely in a blender or food processor. Place the sugar and eggs in a large bowl and beat thoroughly until light and thick. Sift together the flour, salt and baking powder, add the bran and almonds and fold in lightly with a metal spoon. Melt the butter. Fold the liqueur and butter lightly into the batter. Pour into the two cake pans. Bake for 25–30 minutes or until the cake is firm. Cool for 5 minutes in the pan. Loosen the sides and turn gently on to a wire rack.

These cakes can be sandwiched together with apricot jam and dusted with confectioner's sugar or served as a dessert with stewed apricots.

Golden cake

Makes 10 slices

Each slice: 140Cals/590kJ, 1 g fiber

70g/½ cup gluten-free instant potato powder (not granules)
1 tsp gluten-free baking powder
85g/6 tbsp margarine
60ml/4 tbsp golden syrup – measure with a warmed spoon

85g/½ cup soft brown sugar
grated rind of 1 orange
30ml/2 tbsp orange juice
2 medium eggs, separated
butter icing (optional)

Preheat the oven to 350°F/180°C. Grease a 16–18cm/6–7-in layer cake pan and line it with greased waxed paper.

Place the instant potato and baking powder in a bowl and mix well. Heat the margarine, syrup, sugar, orange rind and juice in a pan, stirring to dissolve the sugar – do not boil. Pour the mixture on to the instant potato and beat well. Beat the egg yolks into the mixture. Whisk the egg whites until very stiff and lightly fold into the mixture. Pour into the pan and bake for 35–45 minutes. If browning too quickly, cover with a sheet of waxed paper after 30 minutes. Cool in the pan for 5 minutes then remove to a wire rack. When cold, store in an airtight container in a cool place. Frost with butter icing if desired. Best eaten within two days.

Marmalade cake

Makes 16 slices

Each slice: 160Cals/670kJ, 0 g fiber

115g/½ cup soft margarine
115g/⅔ cup soft brown sugar
2 medium eggs
225g/2 cups all-purpose gluten-free flour
4 tbsp coarse-cut marmalade

1 tsp gluten-free baking powder
pinch salt
¼ tsp gluten-free allspice
30g/¼ cup chopped mixed peel
30ml/2 tbsp milk to mix

Preheat the oven to 325°F/170°C. Grease a 0.5kg/8¼×4½×2½-in loaf pan and line the bottom with greased waxed paper.

Cream the margarine and sugar very well, until light. Beat in the eggs one at a time with a teaspoonful of the flour. Add the marmalade and beat in. Sift the remaining flour, baking powder, salt and allspice and fold in gradually. Mix in the peel and sufficient milk to form a fairly soft mixture. Spoon into the pan and bake in the middle of the oven for 1¼–1½ hours. If the cake browns too quickly place a sheet of waxed paper over it. Leave to cool in the pan for 5 minutes. Lift out and cool on a wire rack. Keeps well stored in a cool place.

Seed cake

Makes 12 slices

Each slice: 90Cals/380kJ, 0 g fiber

85g/6 tbsp soft margarine
85g/6 tbsp granulated sugar plus
  extra for sprinkling
115g/1 cup all-purpose gluten-free
  flour
pinch salt

¼ tsp gluten-free baking powder
1 large egg
30g/¼ cup chopped mixed peel
1½ tsp caraway seeds

Preheat the oven to 350°F/180°C. Grease an 18cm/7-in cake pan and line the bottom with greased waxed paper.

  Cream together the margarine and the sugar. Sift together the flour, salt and baking powder. Beat the egg and add to the creamed mixture. Fold in the flour and add the peel and 1 teaspoonful caraway seeds. If the mixture is too stiff, add a little cold milk, to form a soft dropping consistency. Spoon into the pan and level. Sprinkle extra sugar and seeds on top. Bake for 35–45 minutes or until firm and lightly browned.

Carrot cake

Makes 12 slices

Each slice: 230Cals/970kJ, 3 g fiber

225g/2 cups carrots, finely grated
6 large eggs, separated
225g/1 cup granulated sugar
225g/2 cups ground almonds

¼ tsp ground cinnamon
30g/2 tbsp ground rice (see page 38)
grated rind of 1 lemon
15–30ml/1–2 tbsp lemon juice

Preheat the oven to 375°F/190°C. Grease two 18cm/7-in pans and line the bottoms with greased waxed paper.

  Put the egg yolks in a bowl with the sugar and beat until light and creamy. Mix the ground almonds, cinnamon and ground rice together and blend well. Fold the almond mixture and carrots into the creamed mixture with the lemon rind and juice. Finally, beat the egg whites until stiff and fold them in very lightly to form a soft dropping consistency. Pour the batter into the two pans and bake for 20 minutes. Reduce the oven temperature to 350°F/180°C if the cakes are browning too quickly, and bake for an additional 20–25 minutes. Remove from the pans and cool on a wire rack. Keep in a refrigerator.

  This dessert cake can be sandwiched together with apricot jam and served with canned or stewed apricots or peaches.

Jelly roll

Makes 8 slices

Each slice: 110Cals/460kJ, 0 g fiber

2 large eggs
60g/4 tbsp superfine sugar
70g/½ cup plus 2 tbsp Welplan
  Baking Mix

15ml/1 tbsp boiling water
warm jam
confectioner's sugar

Preheat the oven to 425°F/220°C.
 Line a jelly roll pan (18×28cm/7×11-in) with greased waxed paper.
 Prepare the cake as for sponge tart (see page 83). Pour the mixture into the prepared pan and bake near the top of the oven for 7–10 minutes. It is a thin cake and bakes quickly. Do not overbake. Have ready a sheet of waxed paper with sugar sprinkled on it. Turn the cake over quickly on to the paper. If the edges are crisp trim them off. Spread with the warm jam. Roll up the cake, using the paper to help and keeping the roll as tight as possible. Leave to cool on a wire rack. Dust with confectioner's sugar.

Alternatives For a chocolate jelly roll, substitute 1 tablespoonful gluten-free cocoa for 1 tablespoonful gluten-free flour. Sift the flour and cocoa together and proceed as before.
 To fill with whipped cream or butter cream: roll the cake up while warm with a sheet of waxed paper inside. Cool. When cold unroll very gently and spread with the chosen filling. Re-roll not too tightly.
 Cover with gluten-free chocolate butter cream to make a chocolate log for Christmas.

Chocolate cake

Makes 12 slices

Each slice: 210Cals/880kJ, 0 g fiber

115g/½ cup soft margarine
140g/²/₃ cup superfine sugar
2 large eggs
115g/1 cup all-purpose gluten-free
  flour

a few drops vanilla extract
  (optional)
pinch salt
1 tsp gluten-free baking powder
30g/1oz gluten-free cocoa

Preheat the oven to 350°F/180°C. Grease two 18cm/7-in layer cake pans and line the bottoms with greased waxed paper. Cream the margarine and sugar together until light. Beat in the eggs one at a time, adding a little flour if necessary to prevent curdling. Add the vanilla extract and fold in the rest of the flour sifted together with the salt, baking powder and cocoa. Divide the mixture between the two pans and bake for 25–35 minutes or until firm. Remove the cakes from the pans and cool on wire racks.

These cakes can be served separately or sandwiched together with whipped cream, butter cream or jam. They can be iced with chocolate or coffee icing.

Chocolate munchy cake

Makes 12 slices

Each slice: 190Cals/800kJ, 2 g fiber

115g/4 squares semisweet gluten-free chocolate
85g/6 tbsp butter
1 medium egg yolk, beaten
115g/⁷⁄₈ cup gluten-free cookies, crushed

60g/¹⁄₃ cup raisins or golden seedless raisins
30g/2 tbsp candied cherries, chopped (optional)
60g/¹⁄₂ cup slivered almonds, toasted

Grease a loose-bottomed tart or layer cake pan and line the bottom with greased waxed paper. Break the chocolate into pieces and place, with the butter, in a bowl over hot water to soften. Cool slightly. Add the egg to the chocolate mixture. Stir in the cookie crumbs, fruit and nuts. Turn the mixture into the prepared pan and smooth the top. Score top into slices when nearly set. Chill for at least 1 hour before serving.

Ginger ring cake
See photograph, page 110

Makes 12 slices

Each slice: 170Cals/710kJ, 4 g fiber

225g/2 cups all-purpose gluten-free flour
2 tsp gluten-free baking powder
pinch salt
1 tsp ground cinnamon
2 tsp ground ginger
85g/6 tbsp sugar

60g/¹⁄₂ cup soy bran
15ml/1 tbsp golden syrup – measure with a warmed spoon
85g/6 tbsp margarine
1 large egg, beaten
200–225ml/⁷⁄₈–1 cup milk

Preheat the oven to 350°F/180°C. Grease a tube pan 20cm/8-in in diameter or a pan 18cm/7-in square and line the bottom with greased waxed paper. Sift the flour, baking powder and spices into a bowl and add the sugar and bran. Melt the syrup and margarine and add to the dry ingredients. Add the egg to the mixture with enough milk to form a thick pouring batter. Beat until smooth and pour into the prepared pan. Bake on the middle shelf for 35–45 minutes or until the cake is well risen and firm. Leave it to cool in the pan for 5 minutes. Turn on to a wire rack and wrap in foil when cold. Keep

2–3 days before use for the cake to mature. This cake keeps well.

May be iced with a lemon-flavored candied icing and decorated with crystallized ginger.

Ginger cake

Makes 16 slices

Each slice: 180Cals/760kJ, 1 g fiber

340g/3 cups all-purpose gluten-free flour
½ tsp gluten-free baking powder
pinch salt
½ tsp ground ginger
30g/4 tbsp soy bran
115g/¼ lb (1 stick) butter or margarine

115g/½ cup granulated sugar plus a little for sprinkling
2 large eggs
115g/¾ cup preserved ginger, drained and chopped
milk to mix, as necessary

Preheat the oven to 350°F/180°C. Grease an 18cm/7-in round pan or a large 1kg/9×5×3-in loaf pan and line the bottom with greased waxed paper.

Sift together the flour, baking powder, salt and ground ginger and mix in the bran. Cream together the butter or margarine and sugar and beat in the eggs one at a time. Fold in the dry ingredients together with the chopped ginger. Add about 75ml/5 tablespoonfuls milk. The mixture should drop off the spoon when shaken gently. Pour into the prepared pan. Sprinkle sugar over the top. Bake for 1¼–1½ hours or until well risen, brown and firm. Cool on a wire rack. Wrap in foil and store in an airtight container. This cake keeps for a week or two.

Sticky gingerbread

Makes 12 squares

Each square: 240Cals/1010kJ, 0 g fiber

225g/2 cups Welplan Baking Mix
pinch salt
2 tsp ground ginger
1 tsp gluten-free allspice
1 tsp baking soda
60g/⅓ cup soft brown sugar
115g/¼ lb (1 stick) margarine

90ml/6 tbsp blackstrap molasses – measure with a warmed spoon
30ml/2 tbsp golden syrup – measure with a warmed spoon
140ml/⅔ cup milk
2 medium eggs, beaten

Preheat the oven to 300°F/150°C. Grease a 15×23cm/6×9-in cake pan and line the bottom with greased waxed paper.

Sift together the flour, salt, ginger, allspice and baking soda. Stir in the sugar. Melt the margarine, molasses and syrup gently together.

Gradually beat in the milk. Allow to cool and add the eggs. Stir the molasses mixture into the dry ingredients. Pour into the cake pan and bake for about 1¼ hours, until firm.

Parkin

Makes 12 pieces

Each piece: 140Cals/590kJ, 7 g fiber

115g/1 cup soy bran
60g/½ cup all-purpose gluten-free flour
1 tsp gluten-free baking powder
1 tsp ground ginger
60g/4 tbsp margarine
60g/⅓ cup brown sugar

30ml/2 tbsp gluten-free blackstrap molasses – measure with a warmed spoon
75ml/5 tbsp golden syrup – measure with a warmed spoon
1 medium egg, beaten

Preheat the oven to 325°F/170°C. Grease an 18cm/7-in square shallow pan and line with waxed paper.

Mix together the soy bran, flour, baking powder and ginger. Melt the margarine over a low heat and add the sugar, molasses and syrup, stirring until the sugar is dissolved. Add to the dry ingredients with the egg. Mix to a batter that drops easily from the spoon. Pour into the prepared pan; bake for about 45 minutes or until firm. When cool wrap in foil and, ideally, keep for a few days before eating. Keeps well stored in a cool place.

Boiled fruit cake

Makes 16 slices

Each slice: 150Cals/630kJ, 1 g fiber

140g/¾ cup dark brown sugar
140ml/⅔ cup milk
60g/4 tbsp margarine
85g/½ cup dried mixed fruit
115g/½ cup ground rice

85g/¾ cup cornmeal
85g/¾ cup soy flour
1 tsp gluten-free allspice
1 tsp gluten-free baking powder
1 medium egg, beaten

Preheat the oven to 350°F/180°C. Grease a 1 kg/9×5×3-in loaf pan.

Heat the sugar, milk, margarine and dried fruit together in a pan but do not boil. Stir until the sugar is dissolved; then leave to cool slightly. Sift all the dry ingredients together into a bowl. Add the fruit mixture and the egg. Mix well. Spoon into the greased loaf pan and level the mixture. Bake on the middle shelf for about 40 minutes. If it is browning too quickly, lower the heat to 325°F/170°C. Cool in the pan. This cake keeps well, stored in an airtight container.

Rich fruit cake

See photograph, page 110

Makes 16 slices

Each slice: 250Cals/1050kJ, 2 g fiber

140g/²/₃ cup butter or margarine
140g/³/₄ cup soft brown sugar
10ml/2 tsp gluten-free blackstrap
  molasses – measure with a
  warmed spoon
225g/2 cups all-purpose gluten-free
  flour
½ tsp gluten-free baking powder

1 tsp gluten-free allspice
3 medium eggs
340g/2 cups mixed dried fruit
85g/¹/₃ cup candied cherries,
  chopped
60g/½ cup ground almonds
30–60ml/2–4 tbsp milk

Preheat the oven to 325°F/170°C. Grease and line with two layers of waxed paper an 18cm/7-in square cake pan or 20cm/8-in round cake pan.

Cream the butter or margarine, sugar and molasses until soft. Sift together the flour, baking powder and allspice. Beat in the eggs one at a time with a teaspoonful of flour, beating well each time. Fold in half the sifted flour. Then fold in the dried fruit and chopped cherries mixed with the rest of the flour and the ground almonds. The mixture should be of a heavy dropping consistency; if it is too stiff add 30–60ml/2–4 tablespoonfuls milk. Spoon into the prepared pan and bake for 1½ hours in the middle of the oven. Then lower the oven temperature to 300°F/150°C, cover the top with two sheets of waxed paper and cook for 1–1½ hours more, until a skewer comes out clean. Cool on a wire rack and when cold wrap, with its waxed paper, in foil. Store in a cool place. Allow several days at least to mature.

If this cake is to be used as a Christmas cake, bake with butter and keep for one month well-wrapped and stored in a cool place. One week before the cake is required, unwrap and turn it upside down. Prick the bottom and dribble brandy into it. Cover with gluten-free marzipan and ice as desired.

SAUCES

Canned, packaged or bottled sauces, gravy mixes and brownings, may contain gluten. Use cornstarch to thicken. Many recipes use cornstarch anyway; but if you are substituting it for ordinary flour you will need about two-thirds as much.

White sauce

Total: 350Cals/1470kJ, 0 g fiber

4 tsp cornstarch
285ml/1¼ cups milk
knob of butter

salt and freshly ground black
pepper

In a bowl, blend the cornstarch to a smooth paste with a little milk. Heat the remaining milk with the butter until boiling and pour on to the cornstarch, stirring well. Return the mixture to the pan and bring to a boil, stirring continuously with a wooden spoon. Simmer for 1–2 minutes. Season to taste. If making one of the variations below, stir in the extra ingredients and heat through.

Cheese sauce

Total: 590Cals/2480kJ, 0 g fiber

60g/½ cup grated cheese
¼ tsp gluten-free prepared mustard

Mushroom sauce

Total: 480Cals/2020kJ, 0 g fiber

60g/¾ cup mushrooms, finely sliced and fried

Parsley sauce

Total: 350Cals/1470kJ, 0 g fiber

½ tbsp finely chopped fresh parsley

Fresh tomato sauce

Total: 1150Cals/4830kJ, 9 g fiber

60ml/4tbsp vegetable oil
1 medium-sized onion, very finely
* chopped*
60g/3 slices bacon, diced
1 clove garlic, crushed (optional)
1 small carrot, chopped
340g/1½ cups tomatoes, skinned
* and chopped*
60ml/4 tbsp gluten-free tomato
* paste*

170ml/¾ cup gluten-free stock or
* water*
2 tbsp cornstarch
1 bay leaf
2 cloves
4 black peppercorns
pinch basil
1 tbsp brown sugar
½ tsp salt
15ml/3 tsp lemon juice

Heat the oil in a large heavy saucepan. Add the onion, bacon, garlic, if using, and carrot. Cover the pan and sauté gently for about 6 minutes. Shake the pan frequently to prevent sticking. Stir in the tomatoes and the tomato paste. Add the stock or water. Blend the cornstarch with a little cold water and add to the mixture. Cook, stirring continuously, until the sauce boils and thickens. Add the rest of the ingredients. Cover and simmer for about 40 minutes, stirring frequently. Sieve the sauce, taste and adjust the seasoning.
    Serve hot or cold. Store in a screw-top jar in the refrigerator.

Quick tomato sauce

Total: 420Cals/1760kJ, 3 g fiber

30g/2 tbsp butter
1 small onion, peeled and grated
1 small apple, peeled and grated
90ml/6 tbsp gluten-free tomato
* paste*

salt and freshly ground black
* pepper*
¼ tsp sugar
2 tsp cornstarch
285ml/1¼ cups water

Melt the butter in a pan and sauté the onion and apple for a few minutes until soft. Add the tomato paste, seasoning and sugar. Blend the cornstarch with a little water to make a smooth paste and stir into the mixture in the pan. Finally, add the remaining water and bring to a boil, stirring continuously until smooth and thick. Simmer gently for about 10 minutes. Adjust the seasoning. Serve warm.

Barbecue sauce

Total: 730Cals/3070kJ, 1 g fiber

60g/4 tbsp butter or margarine
1 medium-sized onion, finely
* chopped*
1 clove garlic, crushed
1 tbsp prepared gluten-free English
* mustard*

30ml/2 tbsp vinegar
large pinch cayenne pepper
2 tbsp brown sugar
1 thick slice lemon

⟶

30ml/2 tbsp Worcestershire sauce   *60ml/4 tbsp gluten-free tomato*
                                        paste

Melt the butter or margarine in a small saucepan and sauté the onion
and garlic for a few minutes, until soft but not brown. Stir in the
mustard, vinegar, cayenne pepper, sugar, lemon and 140ml/²/₃ cup
water. Bring to a boil and simmer for 15 minutes, stirring occasionally. Add the Worcestershire sauce and tomato paste, stir and simmer
for another 5 minutes. Remove the lemon and serve.

Spanish sauce

Each 15ml tablespoon: 110Cals/460kJ, 0 g fiber

1 recipe mayonnaise (see page 44)   *60g/4 tbsp finely chopped pimento*
60 ml/4 tbsp gluten-free tomato   *salt and freshly ground black*
  paste   *pepper*

Combine all the ingredients. Store in the refrigerator.

Sauce tartare

Each 15ml tablespoon: 100Cals/420kJ, 0 g fiber

1 recipe mayonnaise (see page 44)   *4 tbsp capers, finely chopped*
1 tbsp chopped fresh parsley   *4 tbsp gherkins, finely chopped*

Mix all the ingredients together. Store in the refrigerator.

Curry sauce

Total: 830Cals/3490kJ, 20 g fiber

15ml/1 tbsp vegetable oil   *1 small apple, coarsely grated*
1 onion, finely chopped   *30–60g/¹/₃–²/₃ cup flaked coconut*
1 clove garlic, crushed   *(optional)*
1¹/₂ tsp cornstarch   *15ml/1 tbsp currants (optional)*
4–6 tbsp gluten-free curry powder   *15ml/1 tbsp lemon juice*
285ml/¹/₂ pt gluten-free stock or   *salt and freshly ground black*
  water   *pepper*
                                      60ml/4 tbsp light cream

Heat the oil in a saucepan and sauté the onion and garlic for a few
minutes, until soft but not brown. Sprinkle in the cornstarch and
curry powder, stir, and cook for a little longer. Gradually blend in
the stock or water, and, stirring continuously, bring to a boil. Cover
and simmer for about 20 minutes, stirring occasionally. Add the
apple, coconut and currants, if using, lemon juice and seasoning, stir
in the cream and heat through.

USEFUL
ADDRESSES

UNITED STATES

American Celiac Society
45 Gifford Avenue
Jersey City, N.J. 07304

Cincinatti Celiac Society
Children's Hospital Medical Center
Attn: J. Lakness
Elland & Bethesda
Cincinatti, Ohio 45229

Gluten-Intolerance Group
Elaine I. Hartsook, R.D.
26604 Dover Court
Kent, Washington 98031

Midwestern Celiac-Sprue Association
Attn: Pat Murphy Garst
P.O. Box 3354
Des Moines, Iowa 50322

National Celiac-Sprue Society
5 Jeffrey Road
Wayland, Massachusetts 01778

CANADA

The Canadian Celiac-Sprue Association
P.O. Box 492
Kitchener, Ontario NZG 4A2

Canadian chapters:

Calgary, Alberta
Edmonton, Alberta
Halifax, Nova Scotia
Hamilton, Ontario
Montreal, Quebec
Newcastle, New Brunswick
Ottawa, Ontario
Regina, Saskatchewan
Saskatoon, Saskatchewan
Sudbury, Ontario
Toronto, Ontario
Vancouver, B.C.
Victoria, B.C.
Waterloo, Ontario
Windsor, Ontario
Winnipeg, Manitoba

Allergy Information Association
Room 7, 25 Poynter Drive
Weston, Ontario M9R 1K8

Branches:

Antigonish, Nova Scotia
Edmonton, Alberta
Halifax-Dartmouth, Nova Scotia
Ottawa, Ontario
Port Alberni, B.C.
Richmond, B.C.
Tillsonburg, Ontario
Windsor, Ontario
Winnipeg, Manitoba
Whitehorse, Yukon

INDEX

Page numbers in *italic* refer to the illustrations.

alcohol, 29, 31, 35
almonds: almond cake,
    112–13
  almond fruit pastries,
    94–5; *91*
  almond macaroons, 107
apples: almond fruit pastries,
    94–5; *91*
  apple cake, 112
  apple cinnamon
    shortbread, 95–6
  apple brown Betty, 88; *81*

bacon: bacon and lentil soup,
    41
  bacon and mushroom
    quiche, 65
  liver and bacon hotpot, 53
baked custard, 87
baking, 32, 68, 93, 111
baking powder, 32, 71
banana bran bread, 74–5; *70*
barbecue sauce, 121–2
beans, 45
beef: beef casserole, 52
  chili con carne, 54–5
  meat loaf, 54; *57*
  steak and kidney pudding,
    53
beer, 29, 31
beverages, 29
blini, *see* Russian pancakes
bran, 34
bran fruit loaf, 75
brandy snaps, 104–5; *91*
bread, 32, 68–74
bread pudding, 90
brown Betty, apple, 88; *81*
butter cob, 74; *70*

cakes, 95, 111–19
calories, 34–5
Canadian muffins, 76; *79*
carrot cake, 114
celery: cream of celery soup,
    40; *47*
celiac associations, 23
celiac sprue, 8–19
cereals, 26, 27–8
cheese: cheese crackers, 98
  cheese sauce, 120
  lentil roast, 62
  Mediterranean baked
    zucchini, 62
  mushroom and cheese

quiche, 65
pizza, 66
spaghetti-cheese in tomato
    sauce, 66
cheesecake, pineapple, 83; *82*
Chelsea buns, 108; *109*
cherry: coconut-cherry
    chocolate slices, 106
chicken with mushrooms and
    lima beans, 61
children: celiac sprue, 12, 13,
    14
  gluten-free diet, 21, 26,
    36–7
chili con carne, 54–5
chocolate: chocolate cake,
    115–16
  chocolate munchy cake,
    116
  chocolate nut bars, 103–4
  coconut-cherry chocolate
    slices, 106
  Florentines, 104
choux pastry, 96–7
Christmas pudding, 90–3
coconut: coconut-cherry
    chocolate slices, 106
  coconut squares, 106; *92*
cod: fish cakes, 50; *58*
  fisherman's pie, 46
cookies, 95–107
corn bread, 74
crisp crystal cookies, 99
cucumber raita, 44
curry: curry sauce, 122
  korma gosht, 51–2
  vegetable curry, 63
custard, baked, 87

dairy products, 26, 27
Danish cookies, 99–100; *92*
dapsone, 20
dates: date-nut squares,
    102–3
  date and walnut loaf, 75–6;
    70
dermatitis herpetiformis
    (DH), 19–21
desserts, 28, 78–93
doughnuts, spicy, 107; *109*
drugs, gluten content, 31
Dutch fruit salad, 86

eating out, 35–6
éclairs, 96–7

eggs, 26, 27

fats, 29, 34–5
fertility, 22, 23
fiber, 34, 35
fish, 26, 27, 46–51
fish cakes, 50; *58*
fisherman's pie, 46
Florentines, 104
flour, 32, 33, 38, 68
fondue, meat, 52
freezing, 32, 38, 68, 93, 111
French onion soup, 41; *47*
fruit, 26, 28
fruit and nut iced pudding,
    85–6; *82*
fruit cake, boiled, 118
  rich, 119; *110*
fruit crumble, 87–8; *80*
fruit salad, Dutch, 86
fruit sherbert, 85; *82*

ginger: ginger cake, 117
  ginger ring cake, 116–17;
    110
  ginger snaps, 102
  parkin, 118
  sticky gingerbread, 117–18
gluten, 10–12, 18–20
gluten-free foods, 27–30, 33
golden bars, 101
golden cake, 113
griddle cakes, Welsh, 77–8;
    79

haddock: kedgeree, 50–1
HLA antigens, 13-14, 20

ice cream, 86–7
intestine, small, 8–10, 11–12,
    18, 19; *9, 10, 11, 12*

jelly roll, 115
jejunal biopsy, 16–17, 20

kedgeree, 50–1
kidney beans: chili con
    carne, 54–5
  kidney bean, zucchini and
    mushroom salad, 43–4;
    48
korma gosht, 51–2

lamb: korma gosht, 51–2
  lamb stew with dumplings,

56; *57*
stuffed peppers, 55–6; *57*
leavening agents, 29, 68, 71
legumes, 26, 27, 45
lemon: baked lemon delight,
   89; *80*
   lemon meringue pie, 84
lentils, 45
   bacon and lentil soup, 41
   lentil roast, 62
life insurance, 23–4
lima beans: casserole, 61
   chicken with mushrooms
      and, 61
liver: country pâté, 51
   liver and bacon hotpot,
      53–4

macaroons, almond, 107
mackerel: baked stuffed
      mackerel, 49; *59*
   smoked fish pâté, 49–50;
      58
Maggie's salad, 42; *48*
marmalade cake, 113–14
mayonnaise, 44–5
meat, 26, 27, 46, 51–61
meat fondue, 52
meat loaf, 54; *57*
melting moments, 105; *109*
mince pies, 96
minestrone, 41–2; *47*
mousse, raspberry, 85
muesli, 78
muffins, Canadian, 76; *79*
mushrooms: bacon and
      mushroom quiche, 65
   chicken with lima beans
      and, 61
   kidney bean and zucchini
      salad with, 43–4; *48*
   mushroom and cheese
      quiche, 65
   mushroom sauce, 120

New Zealand cookies, 100
nuts, 29
nutty squares, 102; *92*

oats, 11, 30
   oat crunchies, 101
   plain oatmeal biscuits,
      100–1; *92*
onion: French onion soup,
   41; *47*

orange dessert, 89

pancakes, 67–8; *60*
   Russian pancakes (blini),
      77; *79*
parkin, 118
parsley sauce, 120
pasta salad, 43; *48*
pastry, 64, 93–4, 96–7
pâté: country pâté, 51
   smoked fish pâté, 49–50;
      58
peanuts: nutty squares, 102;
   92
   peanut bars, 103
peas: green pea soup, 39
peppers: zucchini and red
      pepper quiche, 65; *60*
   Mediterranean baked
      zucchini, 62
   stuffed peppers, 55–6; *57*
pilau, vegetarian, 64
pineapple cheesecake, 83; *82*
pizza, 66; *60*
pork in cider, 55
potatoes, 46
   fisherman's pie, 46
   baked potatoes, 63
   pork in cider, 55
   potato salad, 44
pregnancy, 22–3
processed foods, 30–1
profiteroles, 96–7; *91*

quiches, savory, 65–6

raspberry mousse, 85
rice, 11, 45
   kedgeree, 50–1
   rice dessert, 88–9
   stuffed peppers, 55–6; *57*
   vegetarian pilau, 64
rice bran, 34
Russian pancakes (blini), 77;
   79

salad dressings, 44–5
salads, 42–4
sauces, 33, 120–2
savory quiches, 65–6
scones, 73; *69*
seed cake, 114
sherbert, fruit, 85; *82*
shortbread, 97

shortcrust pastry, 93–4
soups, 28, 39–42
soy bran, 34
spaghetti-cheese in tomato
   sauce, 66
Spanish sauce, 122
spicy doughnuts, 107; *109*
sponge tart base, 83–4
steak and kidney pudding, 53
sugar, 25, 29
sulphapyridine, 20

tartare sauce, 122
teabreads, 74–8
teenagers, gluten-free diet,
   21–2
tomato: spaghetti-cheese in
      tomato sauce, 66
   tomato sauce, 121
   tomato soup, 40
trout in oatmeal, 49
tuna: pasta salad, 43; *48*
   salad Niçoise, 43

vegetable curry, 63
vegetables, 26, 28, 46
vegetarian dishes, 61–8
Victoria sandwich cake,
   111–12; *110*
vinaigrette, 44

walnuts: chocolate nut bars,
      103–4
   date-nut squares, 102–3
   date and walnut loaf, 75–6;
      70
Welsh cheese cakes, 95
Welsh griddle cakes, 77–8; *79*
wheat: flour, 30
   gluten content, 11
white bread, 71–2; *69*
white sauce, 120

yeast, 32, 68
Yorkshire dessert, 67

zucchini:
   kidney bean and
      mushroom salad with,
      43–4; *48*
   Mediterranean baked
      zucchini, 62
   zucchini and red pepper
      quiche, 65; *60*